Book Summary

Whether you are a trauma survivor of any kind or a loved one of a survivor, this book is for you. In *Silent No More*, Gilani carries her readers through an honest exploration of suffering and survival as it affects us all. By drawing upon her personal experiences, she shines a light on the tumultuous landscape of trauma as a whole. The societal forces shaping human behavior across time and cultures. The powerful ways in which we all influence one another, through our worst mistakes and our warmest compassion. How trauma touches our minds and hearts, rendering us as vulnerable to pain and suffering as we are to shared strength and joy.

Silent No More: *An Intimate Portrait of How Trauma Affects Us All*

Iram Gilani

*I dedicate this book to all those who lost their struggle
overcoming neglect, abuse, or trauma, as well as those
who are still out there, struggling today.
My heart goes out to you.*

ISBN Hardback: 978-1-7347679-0-2
ISBN E-Book: 978-1-7347679-1-9

First Published: March 2020

Contents

Introduction: *Whoever You Are, This Book is For You*

"Never doubt that you are valuable and powerful and deserving of every chance in the world to pursue your dreams."

—Hillary Clinton

My story of abuse, trauma, and survival mirrors that of millions. While I am only one voice in a sea of voices, all of our pain and hope blending together and becoming one, I hope that by sharing my personal experiences, I can provide a foundation for anyone reading this book—no matter your age, gender, culture, or past—to reach towards greater ideals together. Whether you've survived many traumas already, are reflecting on your past for the first time, or simply seek to understand what trauma is, this book is for you.

I've faced tremendous tragedies and violence throughout my life, and though I don't consider myself special, I do understand many of the hardships survivors face. I've personally experienced abandonment, abuse, bullying, homelessness, and gun violence. I've faced everything from depression to isolation, poor self-image, and post-traumatic stress disorder (PTSD). At times, I cry. I'm quiet. I get angry. I'm depressed. I laugh. I'm afraid. I get anxious. I scream. And I know the effort to wake up tomorrow doesn't always come easily.

However, through years of abuse, I've somehow found the will to survive and have decided I'm not going to let the negativity in my life define my existence. Instead, I'm going to use it to grow and hopefully benefit others. I want people who have suffered the agonizing effects of abuse and trauma to realize they're not alone. That they are alive and because of that, there is hope. *Suicide should NEVER be an option.* It is a far more common issue than many realize: on a large scale, it is a global issue affecting millions of people through time and across cultures. For each vulnerable individual quietly suffering, it is the difference between death and a new life. And for the loved ones left behind, it is lifelong heartbreak, a loss from which no one can ever fully recover. As a society, we must recognize that we have an obligation, as humans, to look out for one another. I want to provide guidance, strength, and support for people to discover ways to take back control of their lives and find a level of peace and satisfaction, allowing them to rise above where they are today. There are many of us who take heavy steps—silently, and by ourselves—and I hope that this book inspires others to unburden themselves from the weight of carrying it all alone.

I've also written this book for loved ones and caregivers of those suffering from self-doubt, anguish, shame, and the isolation of trauma. I want to help them understand what survivors endure—be it physical or nonphysical types of abuse, forced relationships, violence, et cetera and provide them with options. People who have been abused can feel lost in feelings of silence, fear, and helplessness. Unfortunately, we tend to isolate those to whom we can't relate. By doing so, we can unknowingly cause them further harm.

One of my hopes for this book is to bridge that gap, enabling all kinds of people to build stronger connections and exchange mutual support. A small gesture of any kind (even a simple smile or a wave) can do wonders for those who are suffering. I want this to be a guide for people who have no knowledge of abuse and traumatic events, as well as for the people who have gone through them. I want them to understand that they don't need to look the other way or feel powerless.

When it comes to trauma, there aren't always groundbreaking solutions, and I certainly don't have all the answers either—I am just a person who has learned to rely on myself and make positive changes to find peace with my circumstances. Based on my own experience, however, I've come to recognize things that I lacked in the past that could have made all the difference in my recovery had they been available to me. Throughout the years, I've also gained personal insights that have helped me see trauma in a broader scope: the larger, cultural forces and gender norms driving so much of human behavior; the insurmountable challenges, vulnerability, and desperation hidden underneath some of the most difficult to-forgive decisions; and the universal nature of trauma, cutting across all cultures, worldwide.

These insights, and many more, have helped bring me from the depths of despair to a place where I can grow, and flourish, once again. Most importantly, I've come to know the significance of support. If nothing else, I want this book to establish support for both survivors of neglect, abuse, trauma, and the people who interact with them—which, of course, is all of us.

I want to do what no one did for me; I want to hold the hands of people who are suffering by walking them through their trauma and getting them the help they need to feel whole again. The normalization of abuse towards others should not be accepted anywhere in the world.

1
Silent No More

"There are moments which mark your life. Moments when you realize nothing will ever be the same and time is divided into two parts, before this, and after this..."

—John Hobbes

In many cultures, men are placed at a much higher value than women. From a young age, born into a well-educated and upper-middle class family in Pakistan, I was cognizant that my place—like women in many cultures, worldwide—was to be seen and not heard. I learned my lesson well and faded into my surroundings, trying to fit into my culture and our family's customary structure. Though my family was neither overly conservative nor religious, there was this underlying belief, which they'd absorbed from the larger culture as a whole, that a woman's responsibility is to provide children. At times, women are treated as though they do not even have the right to make decisions regarding their own well-being. The idea of women as submissive is not unique to only one part of the world, nor to one particular time in history, or one group or individuals. Still, it is a serious issue that generates many kinds of pressures and obstacles, seen and unseen, for women everywhere.

One of the consequences is that in many families, sons tend to be the priority over daughters. My father, an only child, was born in 1942. My mother did not have any brothers; only sisters. I did not understand this until many years later, but when my older brother was born in 1976 with cognitive-development issues, my parents' main goal became to have a "normal" baby boy in the family.

My father was a very hardworking man. Dedicated to creating a better life for his family, he moved to Abu Dhabi before I was born. He would visit on and off, but because his time with us was limited, we missed out on the opportunity to bond with him as much as we'd have liked. Meanwhile, my mother was kept very busy caring for young children and other family members, and with my father living abroad for work, they didn't have enough opportunities to bond with each other either. With my father away, except for the few weeks once or twice a year when he came to visit, my mother was put in the challenging position of having to make many of the household decisions without his help.

On top of this, two terrible tragedies befell my mother during this time. The year before I was born, my parents gave birth to their second son, who passed away within 45 days of being born. Their next son died when I was four years old, also passing away within a few weeks of his birth.

The unthinkable had happened. My mother, who had so desperately wanted a boy, wound up losing two sons within a few short years, ending up with me instead. This plunged her into a deep grief: she could not fathom how to be the only parent caring for a young daughter during her recovery. While those around her were sympathetic, they did not know how to offer any kind of emotional support. Unfortunately, for my struggling mother, it was the blind leading the blind. She was all alone in many ways, and every day a mountain of responsibilities, challenges, and sadness grew around her.

In her grief, my mother simply did not have the mental capacity to look after me properly. She did not even have the right kind of support or sufficient time to heal from her own trauma. With no idea what to do or where else to turn, my mother made a decision that would affect the rest of my life: she asked the neighbors, in our joint family house, to take me in as their own daughter—*I was only a few months old.*

I like to believe that through no fault of her own, my mother thought she was doing me a favor by letting someone else take care of me while she recovered. How could she have known, especially in her state of mind, how critical those early developmental years would be for me? How important it was for me to maintain my connection with her, and with the other members of my true family? I do not believe she understood at that time how that one incident had the capacity to hinder my ability to trust and love ever since. She may have underestimated a young child's ability to take in what's happening around her. Often, people believe that children are too young to interpret their circumstances, but this is a myth. As early as two years old, children tend to demonstrate self-consciousness, recognizing the distinction between themselves and others, and gaining sensitivity to what's going on in their environments.

And if there's a traumatic event, a young child's mind will attach to it all of the current sensations—the sounds, sights, smells, physical feelings, tastes—associated with that event. These follow the child through life; so from that point forward, any similar sensations can trigger the memory, bringing the traumatic event right back to the surface. I remember all the key details from my past, although I know that it is in my best interest to not re-live or dwell too much on any of the horrific memories.

I lived with the neighbors for a little over four years, the whole time believing them to be my biological family. Together, we took trips, went sight-seeing or shopping, saw movies, and cooked. We even read books together most evenings. They had another child, so I gained a baby brother, whom we all loved. I had a wonderful childhood with them. I loved them very much.

Then one day, the house was a flurry of activity. I wasn't sure what was going on, but the extended family filled the house, with everybody packing things into boxes and bags. For some reason, the mood felt gray: *was something bad happening?* Outside, a cold winter rain poured down all afternoon and evening.

That night at bedtime, my parents sat at the edge of my bed. They held me, both of them softly crying, and I wiped the tears off my mother's face. It wasn't enough; they continued crying, whispering to me how much they loved me as I fell asleep.

The next morning, I woke up. At first, it felt like an ordinary winter day. Then, as I got up and began moving around the house, I realized I was the only one there. I checked their bedroom: my parents and baby brother were gone.

Panicked and confused, I wandered from their room to our shared living space, where I found my mother's friend, *a woman I knew only as our downstairs neighbor,* waiting for me on the couch. I went to her, crying, and she lifted me onto her lap. She tried to comfort me, rocking me back and forth and telling me my parents would return soon. But when I woke up for the second time that day, I found myself in my neighbor's home, my family still missing.

Again, my mother's friend sat with me. Struggling to find the words, she finally managed to admit the unthinkable: that my family had moved from Pakistan to the United States with my six-month-old brother.

I couldn't believe this. *Why would my own parents leave me? How long would they be gone?* And then, the most painful thought of all...*why didn't they take me with them?* So much had changed in a flash that I couldn't quite keep up with it all and process it. Suddenly, at four years old, I wasn't sure who was going to take care of me. Where I would sleep. What I would eat. When, if ever, I was going to see my loving parents again.

And then, somehow, it got worse. As I listened in disbelief— my world turning upside-down—she confessed the crushing truth that truly changed everything from that point forward. That *she*, in fact, was my biological mother. And just like that, my entire reality shifted.

How could this be? The couple next door, whom I'd believed were my true family, were simply neighbors. The mother and father who had tucked me into bed at night, had held my hand as I learned to walk, had fed me breakfast, lunch, and dinner every day, were not my real family. They weren't *mine*, and I was not *theirs*. For many years, they had been childless, and when my biological mother came to them, needing someone to care for me, they'd agreed to help. When they found out they were moving to the United States, they of course wanted to officially adopt me and take me with them. But my biological parents could not agree to such terms, for reasons unknown to me.

I was heartbroken. Everything I'd known, everything I'd believed in my short life, had been a lie. My other "parents" called a few days later, telling me how much they missed me, and I spent months waiting by the phone for them to call again. They did on occasion, but then the days turned into months, and then years, without a word from them.

Over time, my heartbreak grew into isolation and anger. I'd learned how risky it can be to put your trust in others, and, as my trust eroded, I began losing self-confidence, too.

What Shapes a Young Child's Heart

"Listen to silence. It has so much to say."

—Rumi

Life goes on. Sharing a bed with my siblings instead of the people I'd believed were my parents, was a big change. Their room, which I'd played in many times, seemed foreign to me now that I was expected to sleep in it. We all went to the same school, but whereas my other father had been the one to drive me in the past, I had to adjust to missing out on that quality time with him. This was hard for me. I no longer had the same routine of coming "home" either, because my other mother had fed me herself. Now, I was one of multiple children being fed, and although my biological mother fed us around the same time of day, I missed this special time alone with my other mother.

My other family had been very lively: after school, we'd go out for an evening adventure, driving around in their old Volkswagen beetle or my other father putting me on his scooter and taking me around outside. I couldn't help but miss the fun of those simple and happy activities. My biological mother (for understandable reasons) needed to take an afternoon nap, so she made us all go to sleep for a few hours each day, too.

I'd been fascinated with cooking and cleaning, even when I was only three or four years old and living with my other mother, but my biological mother had lung issues, making it very easy for her to get sick. So, at the age of eight, I started cooking full meals for the six to seven people in our family and taking care of the house alongside my older sister. We could have used the support of our middle sister, but she was a bit lazy and did not always do her part.

Eventually, I became used to the new house rules and familial lifestyle, and even to my new parents and siblings... but only because I had no choice. Though tenderly young, I inherently understood that this was my set of circumstances, and it was up to me to deal with it. I was already learning to suppress my feelings, and fulfill others' wishes of me, because my trust was so damaged that I didn't even prioritize my own needs. By becoming submissive, I could simply do what I was told and let things be. I put my own likes and dislikes aside, becoming a bit robotic in my interactions.

Inside, I felt worthless and unwanted, so I wasn't sure how to socialize or to develop my own personality. I didn't speak about my unfortunate circumstances, because I felt alone in them, and so I continued holding them, all on my own, within. In my silence, I wondered whether anyone would care, even if they knew the truth—in this way, I felt as though I did not exist.

Like the many children who experience some sort of abandonment at an early age, I simply responded to my pain by doing my best to hide it from the outside world by withdrawing, doing whatever it took to get through the day. My school performance faltered, and my biological parents worried about my grades. It was at this point that they decided I could use some help, and they searched for someone who could assist me with my studies.

They hired an elderly gentleman in the neighborhood who agreed to tutor me. Although my parents meant well trying to provide me with some kind of academic support, this turned out to be the second domino in my short chain of life events that tumbled with thunderous effect.

I was sent to the tutor's house most days after school. He was married, but more times than not, his wife was not there during my lessons. He taught other children in the neighborhood occasionally, but somehow, it always seemed to work out that when he tutored me, it was just the two of us, alone. His abuse started with inappropriate touching and escalated to sexually molesting me. I was only five or six years old and didn't fully understand what was happening, but I knew I didn't want to be there. I begged my mother and other family members not to send me, but I was too afraid to tell them exactly what was happening. Looking back, I realize this was as much the result of my inability to understand and communicate about sexual abuse at that age as it was the result of my inability to trust my biological parents. Our relationship was too new and tenuous, and although my parents did the best they could given their own struggles, a child's earliest years in life are extremely vulnerable: what they absorb early on sets the foundation they carry with them forever.

Since so much of what shapes a young child's mind and heart lies beyond a parent's control, it is vital that parents do everything they *can* control, during this delicate time, to build strong bonds with their children and maintain loving relationships: providing guidance and support, listening to the children's needs, and helping them develop their own connections so they can understand the value of relationships.

Years went by, and this abuse continued. Meanwhile, my father, still wanting to create a better life for us, had moved from Abu Dhabi to the United States for work. I wondered: would we ever go and join him? Would I ever escape the abuse of this man? As if that wasn't enough, another man very close to our family, perhaps sensing my vulnerability, began abusing me, too. Because he was so close by, it was very difficult for me to avoid him, and even more difficult for me to imagine trying to tell anybody.

For seven or eight years, these two men got away with molesting me without anybody intervening. This may have been because they trusted these men so much that it didn't occur to them to be suspicious, or because I'd gotten so good at hiding my pain, or both. Besides, given my father's absence, my mother's frequent illnesses, and so many children to take care of, there may have simply been room for certain things to slip through the cracks.

Then one day, we got some very big news: my family was finally granted a visa to join my father and immigrate to the United States! My entire life was changing again. But this time, I could escape the abuse of those molesters at long last.

2

A Hopeful New Start

"No matter how hard the past, you can always begin again."

—Buddha

In all, it took more than a decade to obtain all of the proper documents allowing me, my mother, older brother, middle sister, and younger brother to move to the United States. This meant that for many more years, these men continued to sexually abuse me while I waited, desperately, for us to be able to leave the country. My older sister was married with a child of her own by that time, so she stayed in Pakistan.

I was thirteen when we finally arrived in 1997 and settled in Maryland for a very brief time before moving to Virginia, where we've lived ever since. Being a teenager, there was a lot to take in with the immense cultural differences and the trauma still lingering from the sexual abuse. I was overwhelmed, to say the least. But at the same time, I was relieved to be in America, my abusers left behind. I saw this as an opportunity to start anew.

As I explored my new country's culture, longing to be a part of it, my younger brother grew a stronger commitment to the patriarchal Pakistani ways. Boys are valued above women; their dominance revered amongst our elders. And in our family in particular, my younger brother, who had been born only one year and a half after me, was seen as the only "normal boy." My mother had given birth to eight children: three girls and five boys. By 1997, since three of the five boys had died, we were down to three girls and two boys (my younger brother and my older brother, who had developmental issues). My parents are first cousins, so my mother's father and my father's mother were siblings. When my older brother was born, he had a number of defects: weak eyesight, culminating in being legally blind; hearing impairments, causing him to use hearing aids; a speech impediment; and psychological issues due to improper brain development. The neurologist said he hasn't matured with age the way that others do. In other words, he still thinks and acts like a child.

This led our parents to focus on their other son, my younger brother. He became the center of all the attention—another reason I was given away as a young child without much regard. As a result, he grew up spoiled. He learned to use this to his advantage, doing what he wanted without concern for others. In turn, my parents' love for him clouded their judgment; he got away with everything.

It's very common among the many households where one or a few children receive more attention than the rest, for the prized children to develop feelings of superiority. Often, this comes with unfortunate consequences, such as division—and, in the long-term, possibly even hatred—forming among siblings. To an extent, preferences are inevitable. Still, parents should try to avoid any conscious favoritism as much as possible in order to promote equality and positive relationships at home.

It's important to factor my parents' upbringings into this, too. My mother grew up with cooperative and loving parents who treated their daughters well, sending them to the best school they could afford, where they had opportunities to build careers for themselves. For a few years after graduating college, my mother worked as a teacher but gave up her career when she got married. At home, my grandparents kept my mother and aunts involved in most family decisions, so she grew up with permission to speak her mind. Hers was a grounded household where she had a voice and was well cared for.

My father was not as lucky. His father was the opposite of my mother's father: very strict and demanding, and always making sole decisions that affected the entire family. He was a tough man, difficult to emotionally connect with.

Since my parents weren't able to spend a lot of time together once they were married, mainly due to my father's living abroad, their parenting styles were very different. My mother, having grown up in a collaborative home, tended to include us in decisions; my father, taking after his own dad, imposed his decisions upon us. I wish my father had received the kind of love and care that he deserved from his father, teaching him to love and care for others in return.

As we adjusted to life in the United States, my parents were not happy with my quick adoption of Western behaviors. They saw my excitement and interests as rebellious. At the same time, they supported my brother's efforts to act tough without consequences. It wasn't long before he started to wield his power over me by pushing and shoving, and that quickly evolved into kicking and hitting. If I attempted to stand up against him, then my parents admonished me for disgracing our family with my Westernized ways.

In reality, I was simply trying to protect myself and speak up against oppression, or do innocent things like get together with friends. By then, I was sixteen years old, spending my days going to school, then working most days at the mall until 11:00 p.m. This helped me stay out of the house and gave me a place where I felt safe. Since neither of my parents had gone to school in the U.S., they weren't familiar with American school systems, a large concern for many foreign families. They didn't realize how important it is to participate in activities, get good grades, and prepare for the SAT and ACT to get into a good college. Therefore, our dedication and freedom was confusing and threatening to them. They didn't want me to participate in many things, and they continued prioritizing my younger brother above all else.

By high school, his behavior transitioned to frequent beatings, leaving me with visible bruises. This largely stemmed from the unconditional love he received—he was what mattered most to our parents—and since our family guarded him as much as possible, he continued to believe his actions did not have consequences. In many ways, he didn't know right from wrong; not because he lacked a moral compass, but because no one had ever taught him what they were.

It also seemed that he had a hard time coping with frustration, so little things would sometimes be too much for him. How upset he got with me depended on his mood. This was challenging for me, and while I felt anger towards his actions, I also understood that this abuse was not so simple. My brother was struggling with many of his own challenges. He was a victim himself: both of his own upbringing, and of a social system that had trained him, from an early age, with a sense of entitlement. Nevertheless, his violence towards me was not the totality of him, and that's important to acknowledge.

Although my oldest brother had mental disabilities, he was also a shining light for me during this time. When my younger brother or father confronted me, my older brother became my savior: placing himself between my brother and or father and me, like a shield. I was grateful for his protection against physical abuse, but due to his mental limitations, he wasn't in a position to provide the intellectual or emotional support that I desperately needed. He would sit there, wiping the tears off my face, urging me to stop crying. But he couldn't see within me, couldn't understand my pain, could not understand why any of this was happening.

As I neared young adulthood, I was frequently reprimanded by my father for being "disobedient." We didn't get typical punishments in our home. When it came to discipline, he opted for the extreme, especially with his daughters. I wished he'd given us a chance to sit down and talk things through, trying to understand how his punishments made us feel—they put such a distance between us. But my father had had a rough childhood himself, and he didn't know how to deal with his own children, especially teenage girls. Perhaps his extreme punishments were things he'd experienced himself as a child, growing up with his own strict parents. I could tell that afterwards, he always felt bad for punishing us so harshly.

Between the ages of sixteen and nineteen, he repeatedly threw me out of the house. On countless nights, I'd sleep outside, curled up in a corner, seeking light and warmth. I didn't have a blanket, and since cell phones weren't readily available back then, I didn't have a good way to contact anybody.

This was a scary time when homelessness became my main anxiety, because I was terrified of being on the streets at night, afraid of what might happen. I'd been raised in a joint-family system, where children didn't necessarily leave home right when they turned eighteen, so I was still very dependent on my parents. I was improving my English and assimilating into American culture, still learning to come out of my shell. Many nights, I'd huddle against our family's front door, clinging to the doorknob as I drifted in and out of sleep.

Hearing the word "homelessness," many picture an individual without a home. In reality, there is another form of "homelessness," equally painful and disorienting. Living under a roof, but not feeling welcome there, can be as bad as not having a home at all. This sensation—of feeling hollow and alone, even in the company of others—could apply to anyone who is always on the move, such as military families or to people with unstable homes, like myself. Robin Williams once said, "I used to think that the worst thing in life was to end up alone. It's not. The worst thing in life is to end up with people who make you feel alone."

More than once, I went to school from the street. I'd go straight from my family's front door to the school bus and get ready in the school's bathroom and gym. I used outside tap water (connected to the water hose) to wash my face and rinse my mouth, and in my locker, I learned to store a spare set of clothes, toiletries, and makeup. Often, I was so tired from staying out all night that I fell asleep in class. Due to my brother's physical abuse, I frequently showed up at school with bruises, too, so it was only a matter of time before all of these things caught the attention of the school counselor, who called me into her office many times. On one occasion, she and another woman made me lift my shirt, and when they saw the marks—black, blue, purple—covering my skin, they pressed me to share what was happening. The counselor said she was going to call my parents, but I begged her not to, saying it may only make things worse. To my knowledge, she never called my parents, because they didn't say anything about it.

Inside, I was still hurting from my traumas, and my wounds were causing me to withdraw, to curl up within myself and become isolated. I was learning to become antisocial, and many of my classmates at school, especially the girls, saw me as stuck-up. I became a target for bullying, an issue that remains common among young people even today. The other girls at school treated me as if I were too good to be their friend, but friendship was the thing I needed most. My problem was that I felt so heartbroken inside, so afraid to put my trust in others, that I simply could not overcome this obstacle to connecting. People can be quick to judge others, assuming the worst, especially in group situations. But the truth was that I always wished I had a close friend to confide in about my traumas and bond with. I would have been so thankful for someone who, if they could do nothing more, could at least listen. As more people turn to social media as a form of self-expression, it's only becoming easier to hide our true selves in an attempt to fit in. I did this my whole life, until not being my true self became second nature to me. I grew so good at hiding my true feelings, always with the biggest smile on my face, that people assumed I had the best life. This is something that affects many people, especially new generations from cultures that may feel foreign to their surroundings.

All of this put me in a difficult position: at school, I was at constant risk of being bullied. But I also dreaded going home where I was at risk of fights and abuse. Not wanting to face the students making fun of me, I got into the habit of cutting class. With the mall right across the street, it was easy. I was frequently sent to after-school detention, getting into so much trouble that I was almost expelled. The irony was that detention was a safer place than my own home, so sometimes; I intentionally got myself in trouble so I didn't have to go back. Most days, when I didn't have work after school, I'd go to detention and spend my afternoons there.

One night, when I was a high school senior, I had permission to use my parents' car to go to one of my night classes with a friend. This was at a point when I wasn't allowed to leave the house unless it was for school or work, but when my friend and I got to my house, my brother flew into a rage.

He had wanted the car, and he punished me by violently attacking me in front of her. I think he had become so accustomed to beating me that he forgot someone outside the family would find it wrong. Wanting to protect me, my friend dialed 911, prompting my brother to flee the house. When the police arrived, they saw the marks he'd left on my body and issued an arrest warrant. I was scared to death.

Around the world, honor tends to play a critical role in family dynamics. For the many cultures that believe in the caste system and arranged marriages, honor can be a matter of life or death—many women are killed every day, due to something known as the "honor killing," something far more common than most realize. Honor was especially important in our family, as we belong to a "Syed" caste. Known to be a descendant of our last prophet, Mohammad [PBUH], Syed is one of the highest castes in Pakistan and among many other Muslim countries. In my family, my sisters and I were expected to marry fellow Syeds. This was not a requirement mandated by our religion, but rather a cultural obligation placed upon us by society as a whole.

Growing up, due to how close they were in age, my two older sisters had bonded. They spent a lot of time together and did things as a pair. My younger brother and I, being close in age, had done the same. Therefore, in many ways, he and I had a closer bond than I had with my sisters. In her late teenage years, my oldest sister fell in love with a man who was not a Syed. When my father forbade her from marrying him, she ran away to be with him instead. This had a huge impact on my father, who believed she'd crossed a line. He disowned her, never seeing her or speaking to her again. As a result, he became overly strict with my remaining "middle" sister and me, fearing we'd repeat her actions. My middle sister began spending most of her time outside of school reading novels or sleeping, which left me with even more time to spend around my younger brother. Perhaps this was what enabled us to form a kind of friendship; and also what enabled his hatred and resentment towards me to grow.

Then, when my other middle sister did the same thing, my father grew even more anxious about me and my future. I did my best to convince him I wouldn't repeat my sisters' mistakes, that I just wanted to finish school and build a career for myself. Still, he couldn't help but narrow his expectations onto me. I became the sole target of his pressure, driven by these strict cultural standards that many families grapple with, no matter where they're from.

When the police issued an arrest warrant for my brother, I knew my family was likely to hold me responsible for my role in it, because my actions had brought dishonor to our family. The question was, what would he and my parents do to retaliate against me? By the end of that school year, I found out.

Smile for the Camera

"All it takes is a beautiful fake smile to hide an injured soul and they will never notice how broken you really are."

—Robin Williams

In the summer of 2003, right after my high school graduation and before my brother's court appearance, my family went to Pakistan to celebrate my older brother's wedding. In the midst of all the celebrations, my parents took my passport. To my surprise, they told me that I, too, would be getting married.

It was an arranged marriage, involving a man they'd been introduced to only eighteen days before. I was heartbroken—I had dreams and ambitions, and I felt as though I was paying the price for my sisters' mistakes. My parents said that if I wanted to return home to the United States, then I had to get married and ask for the charges against my younger brother to be dismissed. With my entire extended family demanding it, I felt I had no choice but to give in.

The day we had our nikkah, I wore white and pink. An Arabic word, *nikkah* specifically refers to the marriage contract. It is the official part of a marriage, recognized by Islamic law, where husband and wife accept each other in front of the imam. Later, there would still be another component to our marriage, another ceremony making it official. Afterwards, I went to the bathroom and wept. I felt so helpless, so broken, that I was at a loss for words. Still, I managed to put on a smile for the cameras, hiding my true feelings from the world. Fortunately, most people mistook my tears for tears of happiness. I was relieved.

My husband, who was quite handsome, belonged to a Gilani family (Syed Caste). We were around the same age, and our families shared many of the same values, as far as I could tell. I didn't know much else about him, and we didn't get a lot of time to spend together, either—it all happened so quickly that I was still in shock. I tried to get to know him, but our conversations always felt forced and uncomfortable. I really only had one hope: that the American courts would refuse my request.

However, they didn't, and all charges were dropped against my brother.

Right after getting married, I was depressed and afraid. There I was, nineteen years old and married to a stranger, just to please my family. My dreams for the future shattered into pieces. I didn't want to speak to anyone or to go to school or work. I was numb.

At the same time, upon returning home to the U.S., my family started treating me like a princess. It was as though fulfilling everybody's expectations had taken all the pressure away. The mood in the house was calmer and happier, and I was free to do the things I wanted.

My dad was happy to financially support my husband and me until we became more independent, even offering to pay for my and my husband's education. He also looked at a few neighborhood houses to buy for us. Seeing the change my marriage sparked in my loved ones, I was uplifted. They were treating me better and better. Maybe it was a good thing being married, after all. Maybe I should try to make it work.

We married in 2003, but the visa process took two years. So my husband didn't arrive in the U.S. until 2005. A week or so after he joined us, my family got the terrible news that my older sister had drowned while taking swimming lessons. She was only 25 years old. My parents returned to Pakistan for her burial. When they returned, my husband asked them if he could go live with his brother in New York, since my parents were not ready for the final wedding ceremony, as they had just lost their daughter. They agreed.

My husband and I were staying in different places at the time, so we regularly kept in touch via phone. When he first moved, we spoke several times a week. But, little by little, our communication slowed. There were fewer phone calls, until I got concerned. *Had something happened to him?* I kept calling, wanting to know whether he was okay. I left messages, getting fewer responses from him. Finally, he answered.

"You have the wrong number," he said. "We don't know the person you're trying to reach."

This must be a joke, I thought. I recognized his voice; it was him. This happened a few more times, but he always said the same thing. I knew this wasn't right. Gradually, the truth sunk in, and our communication died altogether.

At one point, we tried contacting his parents in Pakistan and were told that they had sold the house and moved to another country, so no one knew where they were, either. When we contacted my husband's older brother, we couldn't reach anyone. His brother eventually moved away, too.

None of us had suspected that it was all just temporary, that my husband had simply been using my American citizenship to immigrate to the United States. This is a far too common problem, where families in many cultures arrange marriages for their daughters, and as soon as the husbands obtain legal status, they leave their wives and marry someone else. Honor is important, but so are young women's lives. I hope that in the future, families can continue to make increasingly healthy choices for their daughters, preventing their suffering and promoting their well-being.

I can't say I was upset by my husband's leaving, but my family's reaction, and my parents' in particular, was devastating.

They solely blamed me for not keeping my husband happy enough. Every day, I heard that I should have done more to make him interested in me. That I was a disgrace for failing at this. That the reason the marriage had ended was because I'd secretly wanted it to. Many women tend to be held accountable for their divorces, especially in communities like ours.

I was ready to put the whole humiliating experience behind me, but my family refused to allow me to divorce, saying it would bring further dishonor. They lied, telling me I couldn't get a divorce even if I wanted to. According to Islam, they said I would have to wait at least seven years.

It was hard for me to be labeled "divorced" when I hadn't even truly been married. By making me wait, they may have been trying to protect me: in our community, if you aren't married by the time you're in your early or mid-twenties, then people begin to suspect there's something wrong with you. Rumors fly, often leading to depression. If you're in your late twenties and divorced on top of that, then things become even harder. To avoid this kind of suffering, my family thought it best for me to wait a while, hoping that my husband would return. He didn't.

I spent seven years—most of my twenties—tethered to a man I didn't know, all the while remaining sheltered in my family home, where the abuse and degradation from family members continued. I felt trapped, but I was unsure how to express my frustrations without making myself into a target. At the same time, it hurt that no one seemed to see or feel my pain. This was a very difficult time for me. I was in a horrific situation with no way out.

It was not until 2012 that my divorce became finalized. I was 28 years old.

3

A "Random Act of Violence"

"Violence is a disease, a disease that corrupts all who use it regardless of the cause."

—Chris Hedges

During the years of my husband-less marriage, I started earning college credits at my local community college. I took classes, but I didn't really have any clear direction, and there was no one in my life to support my efforts. I eventually quit college altogether and continued to work full time. It was then that I got my first taste of independence.

I'd been working since I was sixteen and saving as much as possible, even as young as ten years old. This was how I was able to gain my independence. It was the key to finding my own place and getting furniture, supplies, and food while looking for a job. Having a few months' expenses covered was a form of security. I moved out of my parents' home and began supporting myself in an apartment. For the first time in my life, I felt on course for the life I wanted, even while managing the stress of the unwanted marriage. Growing up, I was raised to be a rule follower. But I was fed up with the shame others were trying to place on me for my failed marriage, and I started to put my foot down, demanding that I no longer be treated this way.

This was my first time taking control of my life. Now, I was free to rebel against the restraints and expectations I'd been surrounded by for so many years. I dressed how I wanted, attended parties, spent plenty of time with friends, and went on road trips throughout the U.S.

But, just as my newfound autonomy was sprouting, I got into a car accident. It severely damaged my neck and spine, and I had to spend the next two years on disability. I stretched my savings as much as I possibly could, knowing that if I ran out of money, I'd be forced to move back into my parents' house, but it wasn't long before that became my only option. Unable to work, take care of my daily needs, and without any savings left, I had to return to their home and rely on them again.

There I was, right back in the same situation I'd been in before. Only this time, I was even more dependent on my family, and my sadness and depression were growing. It was a major step backwards for me—slipping into a situation I'd tried very hard to move away from.

Around this time, there was another problem taking root in my family: my younger brother sold our family's inheritance, including each of our shares. I'd had plans to use my portion of the money to buy a home or pay for school. But these plans were destroyed through my younger brother's actions, which financially crippled us. Throughout the years, he created fraudulent paperwork and even forced other family members to sign documents enabling him to get away with this. Rather than my parents holding him accountable, they took no actions against him. Instead, they became upset with the rest of us, calling us greedy for having requested our shares. They targeted their anger at me in particular, because my sister was married and independent, while my other brother and I were not; therefore, we only had each other. But the more I tried to stand up for my and others' rights, the more abusive my younger brother became towards me. And when my parents didn't question his wrongdoing, he understood that he was free to get away with taking advantage of us. This made him feel even more superior and powerful.

I was desperate for an escape from it all. After my divorce, my parents had immediately tried to marry me off again, but I refused all their potential husbands. The candidates were much older men, either looking for a second or third marriage or lacking in some important way. Plus, after the betrayal of my first husband, I wasn't willing to marry another man with whom I had no connection, who might use me again.

However, two years later, my younger brother, who had moved with his wife and daughter to Pakistan in 2013, convinced me to come and visit them. He wanted me to meet a close friend of his wife to entertain a potential marriage proposal. I wasn't necessarily ready to remarry, but spending spring break in Pakistan with my aunts and other family members was tempting, so I agreed.

Once there, my sister-in-law's mysterious friend never materialized, but I enjoyed my visit nonetheless. Growing up, I was very close with my two unmarried aunts, and I cherished seeing them in Pakistan, along with my other aunts, cousins, uncles, and grandparents, when they were still alive. I always had fun spending time with them all, traveling and shopping. These were happy visits that made me feel welcomed and safe.

So, on March 8, 2014, I arrived at my aunt's house in Bahria Town, in Rawalpindi, Pakistan, as I usually did during these visits. On March 11, my younger brother and his bodyguard came by and invited my aunts and me to go to dinner with them at T.G.I. Friday's that evening. My aunt suggested we stay home; it was raining, and the roads were in horrible condition. But my younger brother insisted that we go. Since I was only there for eight days, I gave in, and it was settled. Later that day, they picked us up to drive us all to the restaurant. But my brother's car had broken down earlier that day. He claimed that while he was driving back from our family's village home in Islamabad to his house in Bahria Town, that it had stopped working. He requested that we take my aunt's car to the restaurant instead, and then, after dinner, we could drop him off at his car. Something seemed slightly strange about this. The route from Bahria Town to the village home is the main highway. It is almost completely straight, with barely any uneven pavement. As we later learned, his car was actually tucked away in a secluded jungle area far away from our usual route to Bahria Town.

We took my aunt's car to the restaurant, arriving at the T.G.I. Friday's at the Centaurus Shopping Mall in Islamabad at around 7:00 p.m. After strolling through a few stores, we finally sat down to dinner. I sat beside one of my aunts and directly across from my younger brother, facing each other the whole time. I assumed we'd eat quickly, since he usually doesn't care to waste time sitting around after a meal. But to my surprise, when my aunts and I began preparing to go home, he urged us to stay at the table a bit longer. I couldn't be sure, but he seemed to be preoccupied with something. He kept checking his phone and sending several text messages. As we waited for him to be ready to leave, his phone rang a few times, and he left the table to answer it. I couldn't tell if I was imagining things, but his behavior seemed uneasy. I chose not to think too much about it at the time.

Finally, at approximately 10:30 p.m., my aunts and I dropped off my younger brother and his bodyguard, at their car in a secluded area by the expressway, and my aunt proceeded to drive me and my other aunt home.

No more than 30 seconds later, two motorcycles zoomed towards us, approaching from the direction in which we had just dropped off my younger brother. They raced up to the left-hand side of the car and started firing gunshots into the front seat, where I was sitting. They shot several rounds at us, with two bullets entering the vehicle.

According to the police, they fired eight shots at us in total. One bullet shattered my lower jaw, teeth, and gums. Another bullet entered the left breast of my aunt, who was driving. The remainder missed the vehicle. Somehow, my aunt kept control of the car and brought us to a stop. The men on the motorcycles sped away.

My aunt and I were rushed to the closest medical center, the Safari hospital, where my aunt ran inside and screamed that we'd been attacked. But since this facility was more like an urgent care clinic, the staff contacted the police, and we were transferred via ambulance to the Shifa International Hospital in Islamabad, where we underwent emergency operations.

A Waking Nightmare: *The Aftermath*

"They've promised that dreams can come true but forgot to mention that nightmares are dreams, too."

—Oscar Wilde

Although my aunt survived the shooting, she went through surgery and many therapy sessions. Eventually, she began to feel better and returned home. This was a blessing, but unfortunately, my own injuries were more complicated. I had two surgeries, the first on March 12, 2014 and the second on April 2, 2014.

After my first surgery, I was transferred from the intensive care unit to a private room, where I sensed even more tension between my brother and my aunts. It turned out he was upset that the shooting had been reported to the police. Since he worked for the U.S. Embassy in Pakistan, he explained, his job could be in jeopardy if his name appeared on any type of police report or pending investigation. He could even lose his security clearance, or his entire career. Later, I contacted the U.S. Embassy in Pakistan and learned my brother was not actually employed there.

I couldn't speak due to my injuries, but I listened anxiously as my family discussed all of this. My aunts tried to explain that it was the staff at the Safari hospital who had notified the police, not us, but my brother still seemed bothered. My aunts and I weren't permitted to speak with the police ourselves due to our conditions, but according to the police report, my brother gave them a suspiciously vague statement:

Yesterday, on 11-3-2014, at about 10:15 my sister, Iram, and my aunts, [Aunt X and Aunt Y], were travelling in a vehicle number [000] from Ghouri Garden Expressway, between the jungle area, when two unknown, unidentified motorcyclists fired at them. Consequently, my sister, Iram, and my aunt, [Aunt X], were injured and the left side front door of the vehicle was damaged with the bullets. At present I am busy arranging their treatment so I will personally come and file a petition for taking action...

My family and I couldn't help but notice that the statement neglected to mention he'd been with us on the evening of the incident, that the whole meal out had been his idea.

I remained in intensive care at the hospital for almost one full month. During my first few days of recovery, my younger brother told me that his "friend" that I was supposed to meet had been admitted to the same hospital following a car accident. I was in shock: I felt terrible! My cousin insisted she visit him, but every time we brought the subject up around my brother, he abruptly diverted the conversation to a new topic. Since I was still recovering and in a lot of pain, I was not overly concerned about meeting this man right away, anyway. Still, it seemed strange that my brother was avoiding the subject.

While recovering from my first operation, he asked whether I had an insurance policy to cover my medical bills. I admitted that I didn't, and he assured me this wouldn't be a problem. He explained that he had a friend who worked for an insurance company, and that when he'd told her about my circumstances, she'd agreed to issue me an insurance policy of one million dollars. As a personal favor, she'd even agreed to backdate the policy so that all the medical bills could be covered. This was such a relief! I knew what a significant financial burden those bills would be. Still, why would this woman be willing to risk her job and commit insurance fraud, simply to save me, a total stranger to her, some money? It seemed more probable that the insurance policy had been made on my behalf prior to the incident, perhaps when my brother had had access to my passport and travel documents.

On top of this, I came to learn of a transaction that had taken place between my brother and my two aunts a few days before I arrived in Pakistan. Prior to the shooting, he'd asked them if they would temporarily transfer ownership of one of their homes, worth approximately $250,000 in Bahria Town over to him. He was applying for a business loan, he'd explained, and needed proof of assets. It would only be temporary, he pledged. My two aunts had never married and don't have children, so they view me and my siblings as their own. This led them to accept my brother's request. The weekend before I arrived in Pakistan, the transaction was completed, and ownership of the house was officially transferred to my brother.

This was alarming to me. My aunt who worked with him on the transfer has a dominant personality, especially compared to my other aunt. She knows how to handle these kinds of business transactions without confusion or doubt. My aunt had been injured in the shooting, as well. If she'd lost her life in this incident, then it's highly likely my other aunt wouldn't have known how to regain ownership of this property, leading to a situation where my brother could have maintained ownership of the house. Once our other family members learned about this, they made sure he transferred the ownership back to avoid any potential scrutiny from our other relatives. There were red flags popping up all over the place, but it was all speculation, nothing I could prove.

However, since my aunts and I weren't robbed, the police ultimately couldn't find any clear motive for the attack. They decided it was "a random act of violence." Case closed. But the impact of this shooting has been far greater than one random act. The gunshot blew away my mandible and teeth. I've had roughly fourteen surgeries and countless non-surgical procedures. Doctors have taken vessels and muscles from other areas of my body to rework my face, and I've had multiple bone grafts. For the past six years, I've been in near constant pain and, about every three months, I find myself undergoing another medical procedure. Although I'm no longer having surgeries, I'm still in constant pain and according to my doctors, my artificial teeth, jaw, and gums will require lifelong treatments and procedures. No one knows when— or if— my body will reject any artificial parts that I may need in the future. I do know, however, that in order for me to avoid any other major surgeries, I must pay close attention to any alarming symptoms in my health and undergo minor procedures every four to six months.

Still Alive

"Strength does not come from physical capacity. It comes from an indomitable will."

—Mahatma Gandhi

After the shooting in 2014, when I came back from Pakistan, I was angry and bitter with everybody. I never wanted to believe, nor could I have possibly imagined, that my family had any part in this attack. Still, lingering questions about the shooting kept popping into my mind, demanding answers.

Why was an insurance policy purchased through an email address belonging to Smart Start Media, (my younger brother's company in Pakistan, which I believe he no longer owns)? Why was this policy taken out a few days prior to my departure to Pakistan, without my knowledge or consent? Why was my younger brother, his wife (now ex-wife), and my mother added to this policy as beneficiaries? Why had the mysterious "friend" I was supposed to meet— whom this whole trip had centered around—never even heard of me, nor ever intended to meet me in Pakistan?

At times, I shared these burning questions with my family, making threats about taking legal action against them. Each time, I was told to "forget and forgive." I have to admit, there were times when this response enraged me. I wanted answers, and I didn't care how far I had to go to get them. I reached out to congressmen, the FBI, Interpol, and any other government agencies I could think of, even the local police and some attorneys. However, this took a lot of time and effort, and I was busy recovering from surgeries and trying to schedule further ones at the same time, so I wasn't able to make as much progress as I'd have liked. I had to focus on getting better.

The challenge was that I didn't have enough money to cover all the procedures the doctors said I needed, and the more I fought with my parents, the harder things became for me. They said that if I retaliated against them, then they'd hire the best lawyers money could buy, and dismiss any claims I might make against them. I was faced with an incredibly difficult decision: to fight this fight, or put my feelings aside in order to gain the funds I needed to get better. Since most of my medical procedures were considered cosmetic, they weren't covered by health insurance, and I didn't qualify for much government funding or resources from other organizations. So, my parents made a "deal" with me. They'd cover all my medical expenses... as long as I didn't take any legal action against them or tell anybody the details about the shooting.

After working for years, I'd managed to save some money. My dream was to buy a home, and I'd planned on using my savings as the down payment. But my parents said that as part of our deal, I would have to put my savings towards my medical bills, too. Perhaps they felt that losing my financial independence would take away some of my power, and I'd be less able to stand up to them. I sensed this was a trap, but I had an infection that was growing, and I needed money for the surgery as soon as possible.

During my second surgery in Pakistan, the doctors had used my left hip bone to reconstruct my jaw, since the bullet had shattered the bone structure. In mid-summer, once I was back from Pakistan and had started receiving treatments in the U.S., an MRI revealed that my body had rejected the bone they'd used. If I didn't allow the doctors to operate immediately, then the infection in my jaw could cause major nerve damage to my face, or potentially even become fatal.

This didn't give me a lot of time to dwell on my options. It was unspeakably hard for me, choosing between fighting for justice or my deteriorating health. In times of need, many people look to their families for compassion and support; my family was my greatest hurdle to becoming safe and healthy again. Wanting to protect themselves, they used my fragile and urgent condition to their advantage, urging me to make a decision at a time when they understood that missing this surgery would cost me my life. Out of desperation, I gave in to their terms.

Besides my savings, I'd also received $25,000 from the Criminal Injuries Compensation Funds (CICF) and $18,000 from the Letters Foundation, established by siblings Warren and Doris Buffett, to put towards my recovery. On top of that, my parents spent an additional approximate $245,000 on my medical expenses. Although I was grateful to be able to undergo the surgeries, this gave them a lot of control over me, and it was scary to be financially dependent on the very people whom I suspected wanted me gone.

For better or worse, this often included my older brother. For years, I've had to travel to a number of states for medical procedures or surgeries (Florida, Boston, Maryland, and many more). Sometimes we traveled by bus, other times by car or plane. Regardless, my older brother was the only one who'd travel by my side and stay with me during these trips, taking care of me. Due to his own health limitations—his vision, hearing, speech, and developmental impairments—I was often put in the uncomfortable position of sharing a bed with him. I feared that if I slept on another bed or in a different room, then I may wake up after surgery, or in pain, and he wouldn't be able to hear or understand what kind of help I needed. If we shared a bed, however, and I needed to use the restroom or get medicine, then I could just tap him to get his attention.

I was relieved and thankful to have somebody helping me, but the fact that it was my own brother also made me feel exposed. Assisting me in the restroom, shower, and while changing clothes felt inappropriate for a brother and sister. Sometimes, after surgery, he had to help change the tubes collecting fluids from certain parts of my body, and, despite my gratitude, it felt so unacceptable to receive this kind of help from a brother that it left me ashamed. I took care of myself as much as possible to prevent him seeing me in a vulnerable manner, but I didn't have much choice. I was exhausted and under the influence of powerful medication, and I was simply unable to handle myself without his support.

I truly wished that my sister, or another female relative, was present to assist me. Before surgery, I'd speak with the doctors and nurses to obtain all the necessary details on what to do following the procedures so that I could explain it all to my older brother. That way, he'd somewhat understand what to do to help me. On top of the stress I faced going into surgery was the stress of wondering how well my brother, given his condition, would actually be capable of supporting my recovery, afterwards. *What if he gives me the wrong medication? What if he doesn't know what to do when I wake up from surgery? What if something goes wrong in surgery, and I die? We're hundreds of miles from home: how would he handle that kind of situation?*

I prayed to God, pleading for the procedures to go safely.

May God make things easy for my brother, so he can understand how to help take care of me. He always did his best, but being female, I really needed my sister to be the one stepping up and doing these kinds of things for me. I understand it was difficult for her to leave her small children at home, but these were extreme circumstances, where I was in desperate need of her sacrifices. Her lack of support in my recovery was disheartening and angering. I'd been there for her and her family each time they'd needed me. My mother's excuse was that she was sick, and I understood that, as well. Perhaps she couldn't travel as often as my surgeries required. Every two to four weeks, I'd go through another medical procedure, surgical or nonsurgical. My sister could have traveled and been there for me on at least some of those occasions. She ultimately chose not to.

In these circumstances, I just wasn't in a position to get a job or move out, so I found myself unable to gain back my former independence. All I could do was pray, doing my best to stay strong in spite of the miserable circumstances. School became my best escape route, and I took advantage of it, diving into academics with full force. I didn't mind what I was studying, as long as I had a place to go where I was safe and welcome anytime I was feeling overwhelmed by being at home.

Many people go through traumas, so they understand how things such as abandonment, betrayal, and grief can make it feel as though the world is shifting underneath your feet. For me, no matter what challenges I faced, no matter how uncertain things became, I always had my body to count on, my physical self, my refuge. It was the only sanctuary that had remained consistent throughout my life. The shooting breached this final, personal sphere, violating me in a way I'd never known before, leaving me completely disoriented.

Since I lost my lower teeth and gums, I also lost the ability to laugh... *forever.* The muscle damage stopped my lower mouth from moving in accordance with my upper lip, and I have a mouthpiece, which contains artificial teeth and gums that the doctors can only make look so realistic. Makeup helps but can't cover it up completely, and the nerve damage has left me in frequent pain—a sharp, stabbing pain that comes from out of nowhere. I've also lost a lot of sensation around my jaw, so washing my face hurts. Putting on lotion, makeup, and clothes hurts. It is challenging to "forget and forgive" something you are frequently reminded of through jolts of pain. Anytime I look in the mirror, I come face-to-face with what has happened to me. And when I leave the house, others are confronted by it, too.

For a while, after the shooting, I'd fall asleep at night in tears, asking God to take this pain away from me, to relieve me of these deformities and scars. *Please, God, let this be the longest and worst nightmare of my life, and nothing more.* I didn't have friends or family I could reach out to who understood how to empathize or listen. And even if I had, I wouldn't have been sure how to open up with them, regardless. I was still in the habit of suppressing my pain, worried that there wasn't enough "room" for my problems, that I'd inconvenience others with my "nonsense."

I knew, deep down, that something was seriously wrong, but I couldn't figure it out. All I knew was I was overly emotional all the time. I was also becoming extremely sensitive to everything in my surroundings. The slightest sight, sound, or sensation made me burst into tears, even if it had nothing to do with my injuries. My heart would race a thousand miles an hour. I'd go freezing cold, yet my entire body would be buried in sweat. My emotions ran away from me, coming out at unpredictable times and in ways I couldn't explain. One day, I'd be enraged, screaming at the top of my lungs like a crazy person. Another day, I'd laugh and cry at the same time. I was so confused about it all that sometimes, after calming down, I felt as though I'd truly scared myself.

None of it made sense. I didn't know why I was feeling these things so spontaneously and in such extremes. I tried doing online research, but too many websites popped up, mentioning everything from bipolar to depression to PTSD, and my symptoms seemed to match all three. This spiraled me into a deeper depression. *Not only am I suffering from physical pain,* I thought. *But I may also have a disorder and cannot get help.*

I came to understand that I was facing more than just depression, but I also knew that without proper treatment and care, I was unable to get the help I needed to get to the bottom of it. Unfortunately, the only suggestion anyone knew to make was to see a therapist. I would have liked that, but I couldn't afford the co-pay. And my parents were already overwhelmed from my many medical expenses as it was, so I felt that I couldn't ask them for more money. I was concerned that they saw me as a burden. That they believed I may be the root cause of all these problems. That they may secretly wish I'd just die already. Asking them for more help would simply be taking too big a risk. What if they told me to leave the house again?

This sparked an even deeper change in who I was. When I lost my physical appearance, I also lost the ability to withstand abuse; I felt that others were going too far with the way they treated me, and I could no longer tolerate it. My entire personality did a 180. I went from being a sweet, submissive girl to refusing to let anybody tell me how to live my adult life anymore.

During this time, things were shifting in a way that started to help me gain some power over my circumstances: my parents were growing older, and I was slowly becoming more aware of my rights. Also, my sister's youngest child was born a little over a month after the shooting, so although I was struggling with deep depression, it was a joy to be able to spend time with someone so new to the world—she was only a few months old when I first met her.

I love children, and spending time with her was a healthy distraction from my pain. I fed her, bathed her, changed her clothing, changed her diapers, and more. Whatever she needed, I made sure to provide, as a way to keep myself busy. A beautiful bond formed between us, something I desperately needed. She became my greatest motivation to recover, as well. As she grew up, starting to understand her surroundings and how to speak, she grew into a very curious child, asking me all kinds of questions. Trying my best to hold in my tears, I'd tell her I was in an accident. Sometimes I'd cry, and she'd wipe my tears away with her tiny hands or kiss my scars. She'd softly touch my face, telling me I'm pretty. These tiny acts of love and kindness became my everything; the perfect motivation for me to heal.

I was still struggling, and I hadn't forgotten any of the events that scarred my past, but I was beginning to believe that I was strong enough to not take any more abuse. I was going to find a way to take full control of things.

The truth was that I was my only advocate. If I wanted to get better, there was no one who could make that happen but me. Somehow, I had to be the one to fill myself with the strength and encouragement to climb out of this.

Photo Section: *Memories are Forever*

WARNING: *This section contains images that some viewers may find disturbing. Viewer discretion advised.*

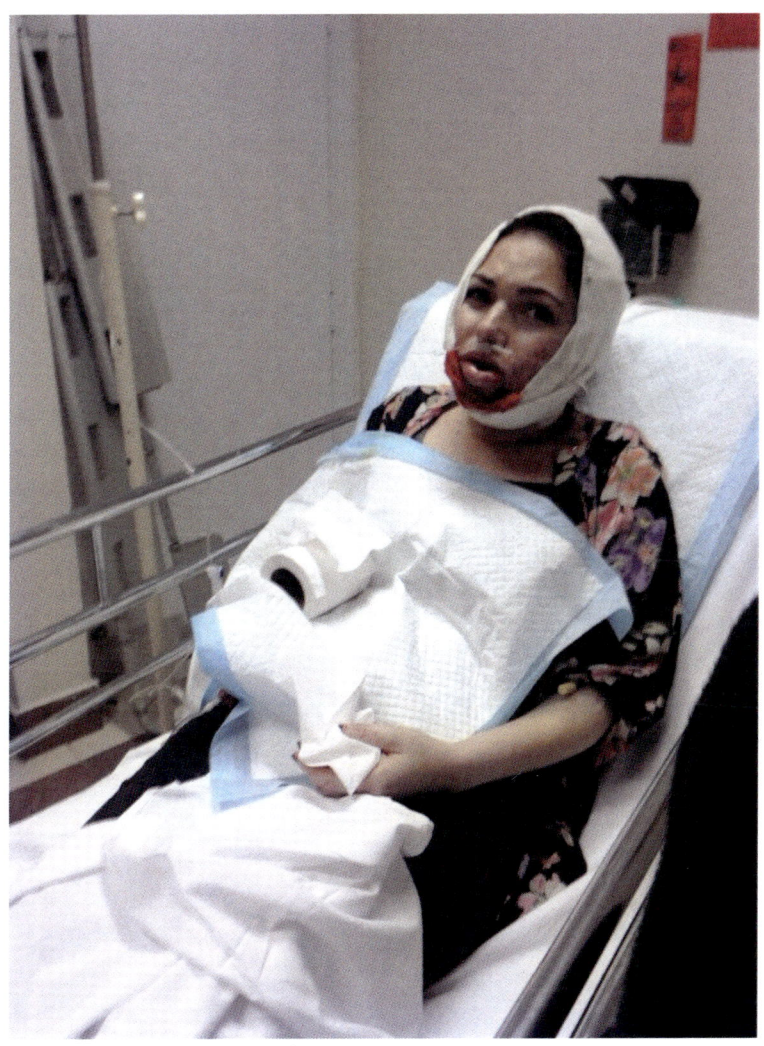

March 11, 2014 - Shifa International Hospital - Islamabad,
Pakistan - Immediately After Shooting

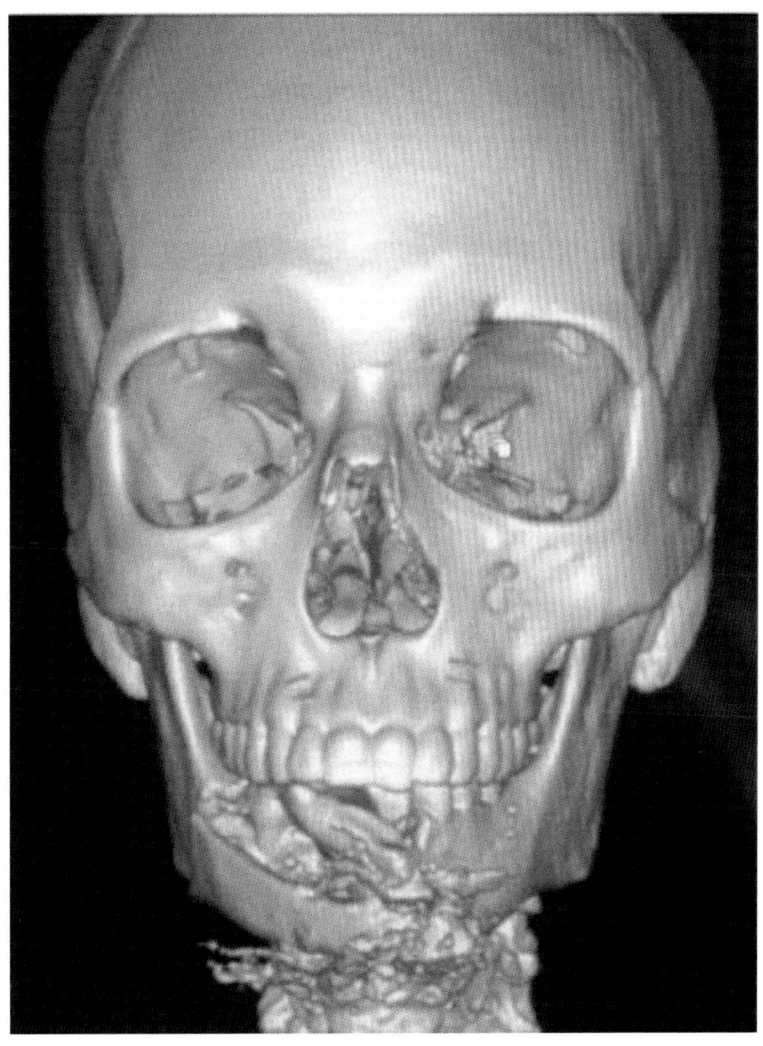

March 12, 2014 - Shifa International Hospital - Islamabad,
Pakistan - X-Ray of Mandible 1

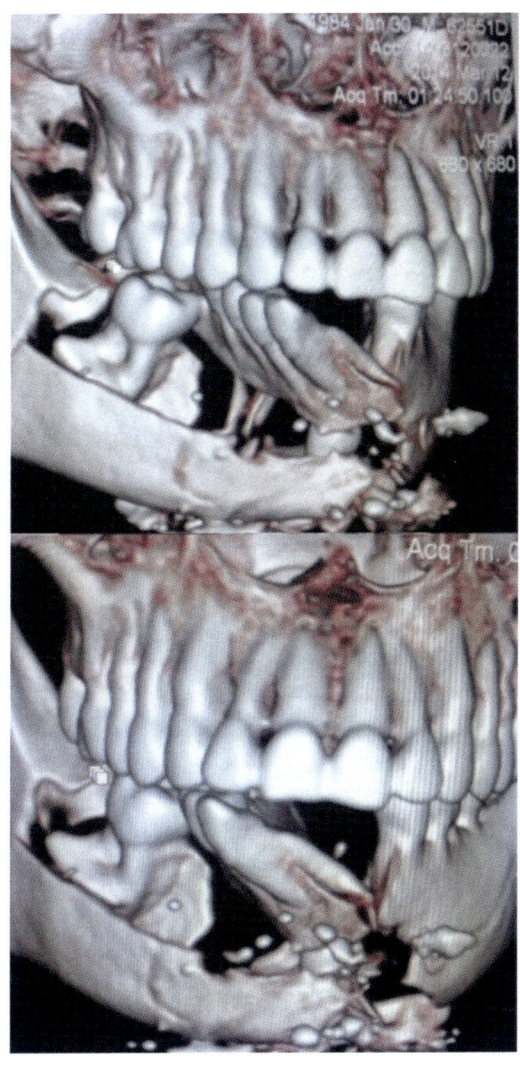

*March 12, 2014 - Shifa International Hospital - Islamabad,
Pakistan - X-Ray of Mandible 2*

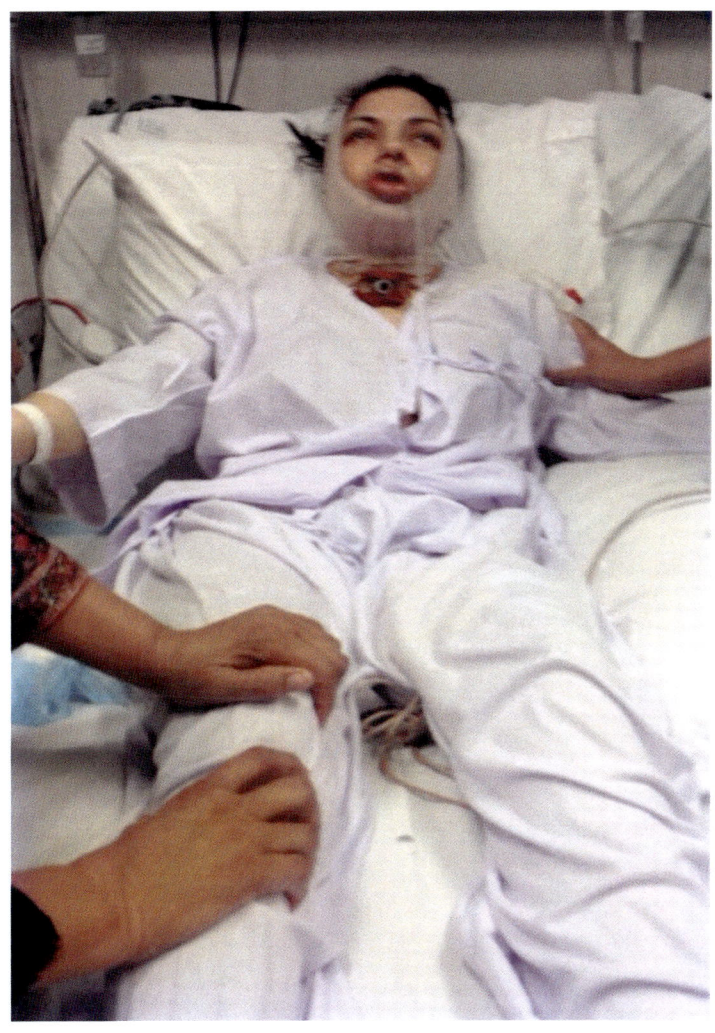

March 12, 2014 - Shifa International Hospital - Islamabad, Pakistan - Intensive Care - First Surgery

March 2014 - Islamabad, Pakistan - Car Exterior

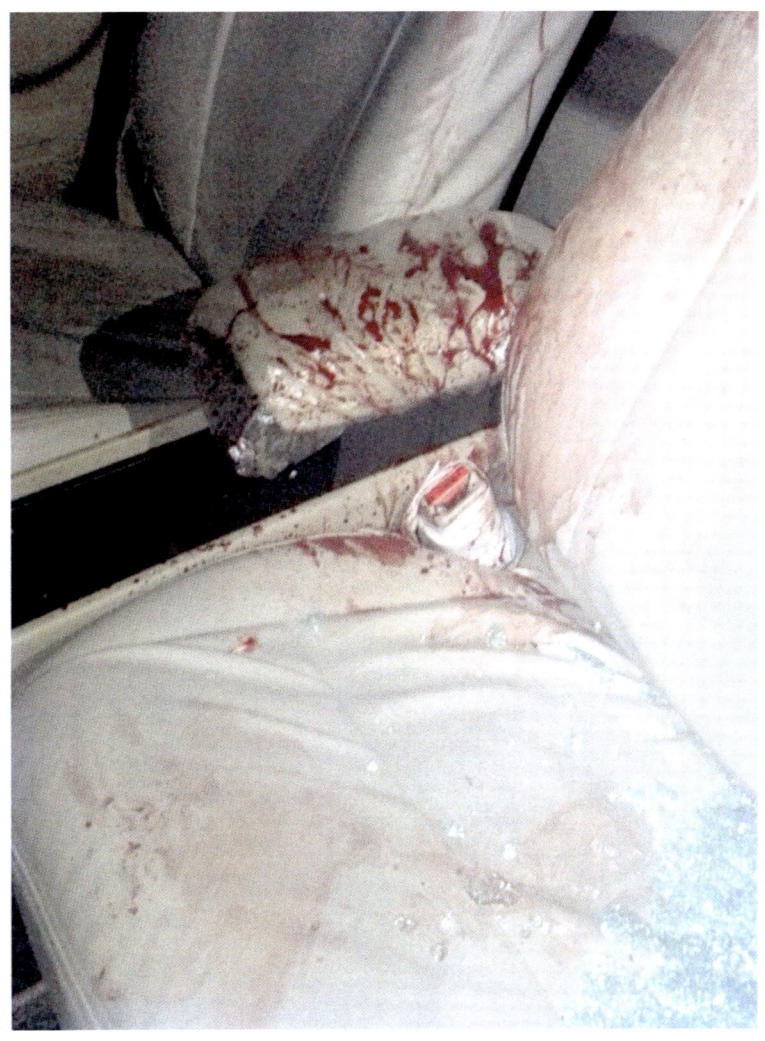

March 2014 - Islamabad, Pakistan - Car Interior

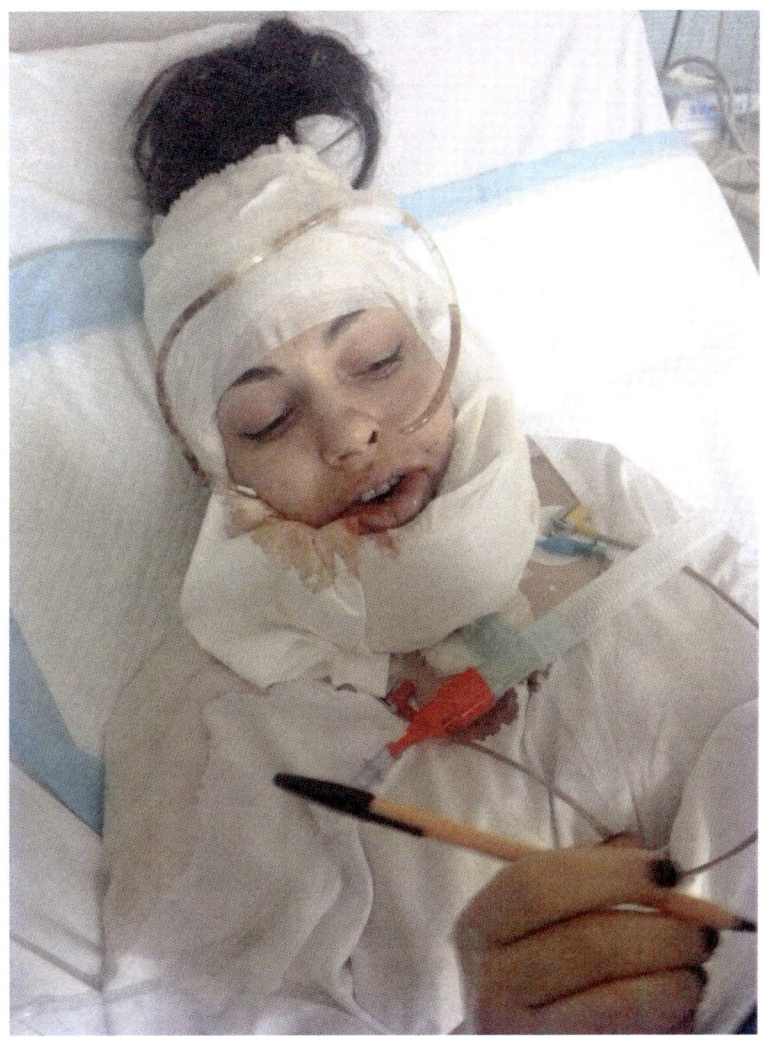

March 2014 - Shifa International Hospital - Islamabad,
Pakistan - First Surgery

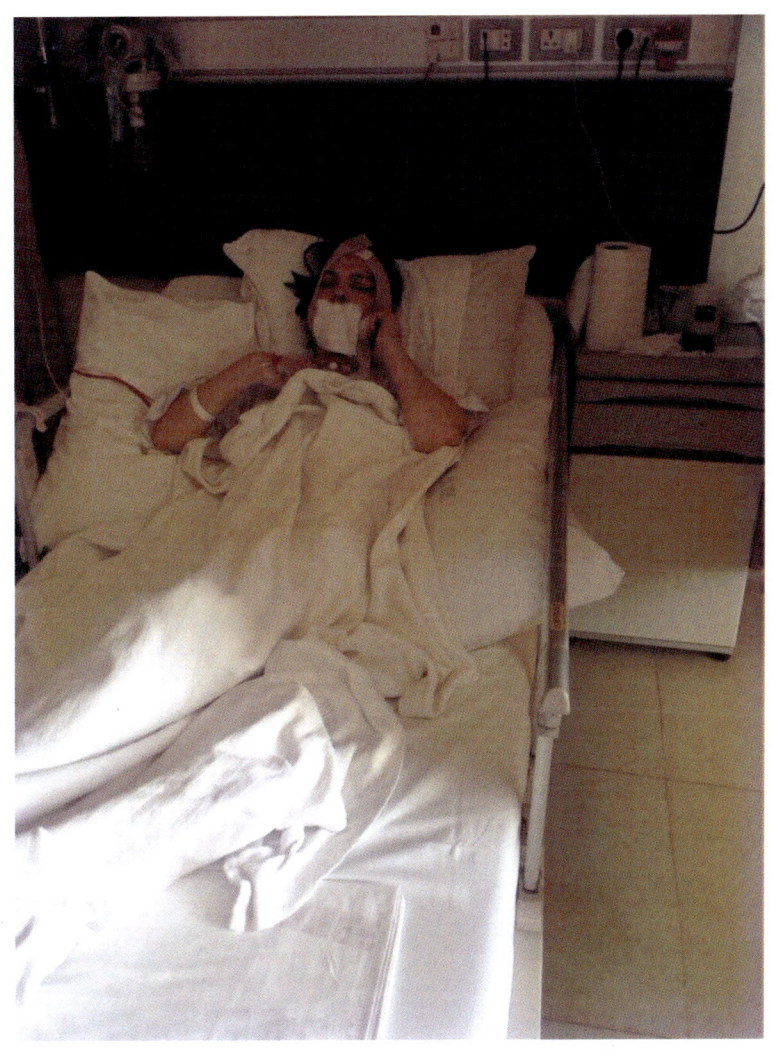

March 2014 - Shifa International Hospital - Islamabad,
Pakistan - Second Surgery

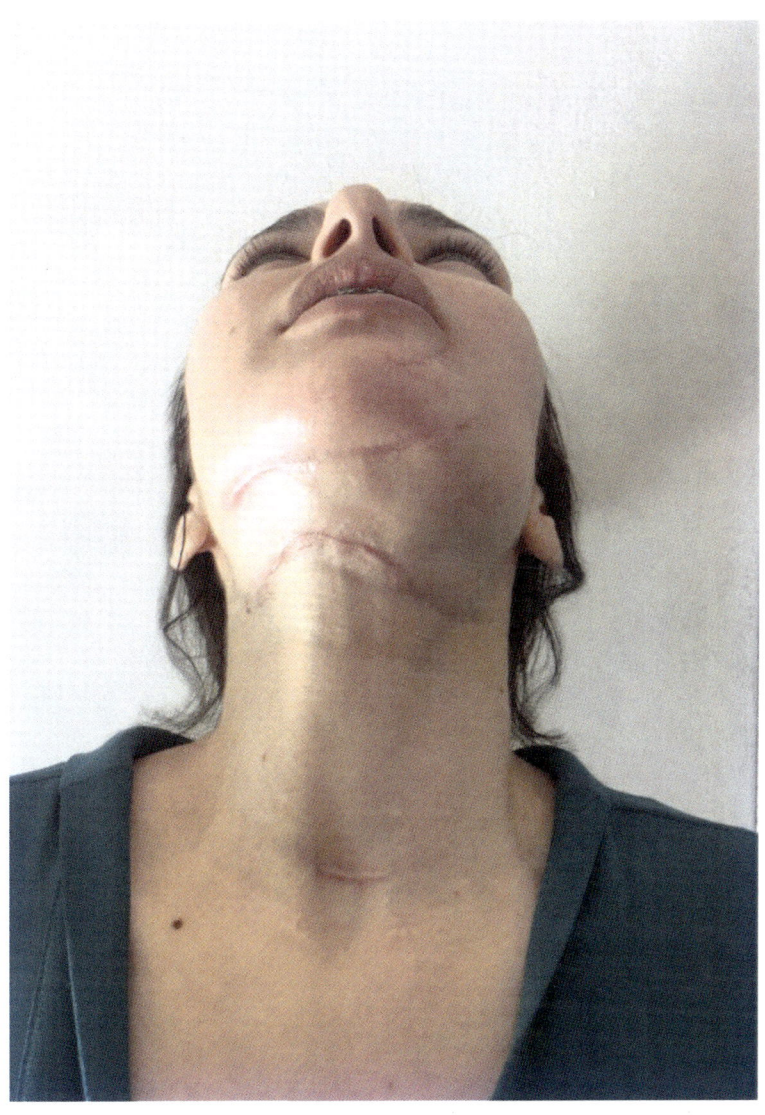

July 26, 2016 - Virginia, U.S. - At Home - Eighth Surgery

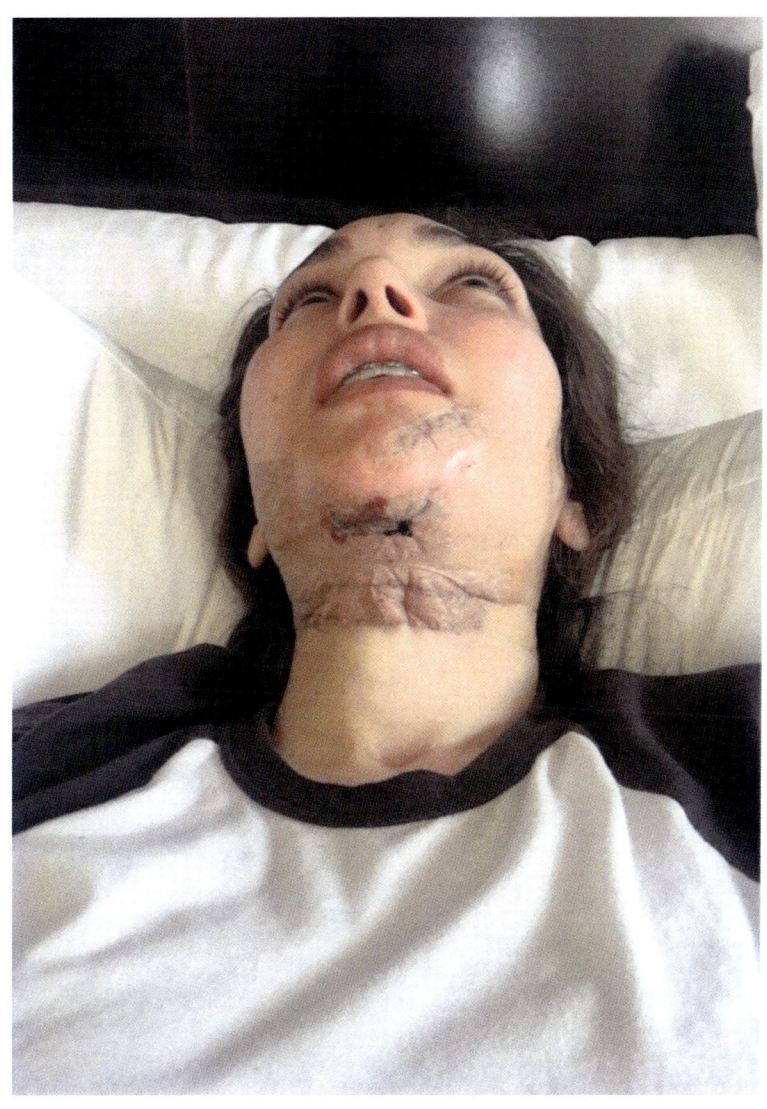

August 15, 2017 - Florida, U.S. - Eleventh Surgery

*May 16, 2019 - Washington, D.C. - George Washington
University Graduation*

February 21, 2020 - Virginia, U.S. - At Home - My Older Brother and me

4

Miserable Doesn't Equal Broken

"Every moment wasted looking back keeps us from moving forward."

—Hillary Clinton

There is no arguing that I've experienced a number of unfortunate events in my life—abandonment, childhood molestation, physical abuse, forced marriage, and gun violence. I've suffered so many traumas, day in and day out, from such a young age that I've come to understand a form of anguish and despair I'd wish on no other. But the worst part of it all was the feeling that I was alone in my pain, that it was up to me to carry it on my shoulders. I believe those around me would have liked to have been helpful, they simply didn't know how. This has made me appreciate the role of support in overcoming problems.

My biological parents could never have guessed that entrusting another couple with my care as a young child could have such long-term consequences. I've always found it difficult to trust others, so I haven't known how to form and maintain close relationships as I've matured. To this day, I worry that people may disappear from my life at any moment. But that diminished trust wasn't even my greatest challenge. It was the loneliness I felt, since no one around me knew how to support me: any kind of psychological, physical, or emotional comfort that anyone could have offered would have meant a lot to me and made a huge difference in my recovery. This was the largest hurdle for me to overcome.

There were times when I cried all day, because I thought no one cared. I never confessed the molestations to my family, but their physical and verbal abuse towards me was out in the open, as were my medical traumas. Yet, they seemed to wish I'd simply accept these things, forgetting that they'd ever happened. I wished I could too, but that isn't realistic. Trauma cannot simply go away on its own. Still, ever since the shooting, I've endured daily pain and constant surgeries, and the belief of those around me has been: *the event happened six years ago, is it not possible to put my focus on something else?*

My younger brother and his wife moved back to the United States from Pakistan shortly after the shooting. When my parents allowed them to move in with us, I was shocked. I couldn't believe my parents thought this was a good idea after what I'd gone through with the shooting and my brother's physical abuse while I was growing up. I was unable to work, because I was going through one surgery after another, and I was in so much pain. I was dependent on my parents and living in their home, and they moved my tormentor right into the home with us. It was unbelievable to me.

In order to keep the peace in the household, my parents urged me to pretend that everything was fine, and always has been. It hurt that they were willing to pretend the past did not exist. I want them, and everyone, to understand that when a person suffers a traumatic event, it's just not that easy to move on. As much as I wish there was a quick and magical solution, there isn't.

Every time I hear the words "forgive and forget," anger courses through my body. I can be in a perfectly good mood, enjoying time with my nieces and nephew, and in a split second, be a different person. These kinds of statements plunge my body into enormous changes. And, coupled with my family's lack of support, they can make it very difficult for me to heal. Knowing that my parents are close by and that they lack the ability to support me during these vulnerable moments has made it difficult for me to fully heal. I've come to realize these as symptoms of post-traumatic stress disorder (PTSD).

For as long as I can remember, I associated PTSD with veterans. I saw it as a condition that affected people in war zones; it couldn't possibly have anything to do with someone like me. But the first time I examined the details, I could hardly believe it—the way I felt in the presence of someone who has harmed me was a telltale sign. I realized that there must be so many other people, just like me, who don't understand what is happening to their minds, hearts, and bodies when they experience PTSD-related episodes. For me in particular, this explained the stress I felt when I was around my family, and anytime something small happened to trigger my anxiety...even if someone closed a door too loudly, the sound made me jump out of my skin.

This reaction was not limited to only my brother or family. My sexual abuse and the betrayal of my husband had weakened my ability to trust men in general and build relationships with them. The very thought of getting married or having a relationship scared me to death. The possibility of getting hurt again was more than I could bear; it was as though life was being sucked out of my body. To this day, I have a very difficult time being around men, a challenge many others can relate to for their own individual reasons.

For those who are fortunate enough to have not experienced this kind of trauma, these emotional and physical responses can be hard to understand. Survivors can't just close a door to the incident that traumatized them, because it runs far deeper than one traumatic moment in time. Much more than my face was shattered, and every person who suffers trauma knows what I mean. Others should take the time to understand the underlying effect that abuse and trauma has on a sufferer. It's a long road to seeing hope at the end.

Moreover, the lack of understanding about the effects of abuse and trauma only prolongs those effects. Survivors need far more than casual encouragement; they deserve physical and emotional support for however long they may need it. They need kindness and a listening ear. In particular, family and friends closest to the survivor are in an ideal position to provide compassion, in as many ways as they know how.

A Path to Self-Preservation

"If you are still looking for that one person who will change your life, take a look in the mirror."

—Roman Price

Empathy is not culturally specific. And empathy and support are what every survivor of abuse or trauma depends on for recovery. When it is in short supply or unavailable, it's difficult to move forward.

There was a time when I felt like the unluckiest person in the world, because I didn't have one single person I could lean on. I felt like no one understood what I was going through. Beyond the high school guidance counselor, I never sought professional help due to lack of insurance and finances. Early on, I was also hindered by a language barrier, and I didn't know of other culturally-appropriate services that existed. And well-meaning friends often weren't able to connect with the depth of my struggles, through no fault of their own.

I could have easily let depression rule my life. At nineteen, shortly after I was forced into marriage and my husband left, I thought my life was over. I spent several months ignoring my responsibilities. I wanted to numb my feelings and anger towards my parents by putting them through a bit of the suffering I was bearing.

There were also the days when I had absolutely no will to get out of bed. I simply wanted to disappear in the warmth of my cocoon and let the world go on without me. I also succumbed to doing what I was ordered to do. If I was told to sit there, I did. If I was told to get a glass of water, I did. I just went along with everybody's wishes. I had no personal say in anything, and this grew into a complete lack of engagement with the world. Even today, I must fight against the urge to hide away or just say yes or stay silent, because this is the less painful route.

But I do resist.

At some point, I saw through the fog of pain and realized my life was far from over. I recognized that without the support of family or others, I needed to depend on myself. If I wanted to move forward, then I needed to find the motivation to do so, because no one else was going to do it for me.

I grasped the fact that, through isolation, I was only letting my anguish predominate my existence. It was I who was letting my peers move on to careers and families while I stayed mired in dependence. Yes, I've been abused. Yes, I've suffered traumatic events. Yes, I struggle to feel whole. But *no*, my life isn't meaningless or without opportunity.

I've struggled with depression and felt miserable, but, through these, I've also found a reserve of self-preservation and personal growth. After my divorce was finalized in 2012, I said: *My life isn't over. I can move forward. And I'm not going to let those around me who choose to hurt me with words, fists, and harmful actions win.*

Not Powerful Enough to Break Me

"There is nothing stronger than a broken woman who has rebuilt herself."

—Hannah Gadsby

I returned to school. It wasn't easy, but I decided to turn the negativity in my life into something useful. I had to force myself to have the will to do what was right for me. I've made mistakes along the way too...all part of the process.

Today, I'm just starting a career, whereas others my age have fifteen years of experience in theirs. I slumped into severe depression after the shooting and had to resurrect my commitment to personal wellbeing. It's been a struggle to face each day, but after six years, through perseverance and daily affirmations, I completed my education at George Washington University. I continued to dream of a new tomorrow.

I'm proud of the determination and personal motivation I showed. I sought out what I lacked from family and close friends. Again, I couldn't afford professional help due to my astronomical medical bills, but I did the next best thing. I read.

Whenever I got my hands on inspirational and motivational stories, I absorbed them. When I found a quote that particularly spoke to me, I wrote it down on a sticky note. I literally had, and still have, hundreds of sticky notes stuck around my room or in my car, and any place where I'd be sure to see them throughout the day: in my books, on my laptop, and especially on my mirror. My self-made support system consisted of Robin Williams, Oprah

Winfrey, Hillary Clinton, Ellen DeGeneres, Maya Angelou, and many others.

I journaled and kept myself busy with more productive things like working and going to school. I took more credits than I needed to graduate, because classes were a refuge from the onslaught of my otherwise daily pain and mistreatment. And lastly, I reminded myself regularly that I wasn't going to let those who wanted to keep me silent and suffering win.

I was angry and resentful about a lot of the things that had taken place, but I was no longer going to give them an opportunity to overtake my life or destroy me. For the longest time, I was stuck on making my family understand how physically, mentally, and emotionally difficult it was for me to heal on my own without enough support from others. But, try as I might, I couldn't force them to recognize something they didn't understand. And in the process, I was only making myself feel worse. I didn't want to give them even more power over me by making them focus on the amount of influence their actions had on my life. I didn't want them to believe that they were powerful enough to break me; I wanted them to see that no matter what threats or obstacles the world threw at me, that I was strong enough to either withstand or repel them.

I chose to deflect and rise again. With self-motivation (because I was getting none from my family), I decided that if others can do it, so can I. And in the end, I believe that if I can inspire even one person to survive whatever life throws their way, then nothing I've endured will have been in vain.

5

Stronger Than You Think

"When I look back on my life, I see pain, mistakes, and heartache. When I look in the mirror, I see strength, learned lessons, and pride in myself."

—Vaidehi Borkar

As I've learned to cope with challenges, I've found that a few particular techniques have helped me overcome limiting beliefs, maintain positive momentum, and connect with my innermost feelings, bringing me closer to the kind of future I want to have.

These are not instructions, but potential starting points for your own path. Take to heart the ones that feel most useful to you and if it helps, share them with others. The best thing about them is that they're accessible to everybody. So no matter your story, and whatever your goals, I encourage you to take full advantage of these six tips that have given so much to me throughout my own recovery.

Tip #1: Hope Burns Eternal

"Strength doesn't come from what you can do. Strength comes from overcoming the things you thought you couldn't."

—Rikki Rogers

One of my earliest and most successful survival strategies (although I didn't know it until recently) dates back to when I was only four or five years old. It was simply keeping hope that things could get better. From my early abandonment and sexual molestation, I didn't lose faith that my circumstances could improve one day. I simply kept striving for better things. Hope burns eternal, after all, and there's always a tomorrow.

For years, as a child in Pakistan, I drifted through a maze of grief, confusion, and suffering. But when my family's immigration documents were finalized, and we moved to the United States, my hope for a new start was reborn. After my forced marriage, the severe car accident, the divorce... each time, I simply restarted again. During those periods, I was not immune to other struggles. My family's verbal and emotional abuse escalated, and other tragedies still found their way to me, but each time, I eventually found the hope to continue onwards.

One of the greatest challenges I faced in restarting was after the shooting. For much of that time, I hid away, only going out for classes and work. That was due in large part to the daily pain and visible reminders of violence against me. It's only been recently that I started to go out with friends. Yet here I am, restarting again as a college graduate, author, and advocate for fellow survivors. I still don't feel like I am where I want to be in life, but I'm hopeful that I'm on the right track, and that's enough. I don't know what the future holds, but I know I'm on the path to making positive changes and independence, and that if another roadblock reveals itself, I'll always have the ability to readjust and start my journey again.

Tip #2: Journal

"Journaling is like whispering to one's self and listening at the same time."

—Mina Murray

Many experts have communicated the benefits of daily reflection. I can only add that for me, daily journaling has helped me detail my thoughts and make sense of my abuse and trauma. Along the way, it became more about recording inspiration and capturing motivation. It was then that journaling held the greatest rewards for me.

I wrote letters to my abusers, expressing my anger towards them, imagining they could understand my pain, just once, and help with my recovery. I never gave them the letters, but the mere act of expressing all this through writing brought me some relief. Each time I felt myself becoming sad or scared, I wrote letters to myself, reminding me of all the happy times I've experienced despite the bad times. I worked hard to commit these happy details to memory, refusing to let them fade. I encouraged myself that my life holds value, and that I'm blessed. That I am here because God wants me to be here, and if He keeps getting me up each day, there must be a reason, even if it lies beyond my understanding.

As a small child, I'd been neat and tidy, keeping everything in place and taking care of my belongings. I didn't throw clothes on the floor or keep things lying around. I wouldn't even leave home without cleaning my room first. The shooting changed this; I forgot how much it meant to me to keep my surroundings in order. Everything in my life was in shambles, both inside and out. It felt like I was just counting the days and waiting to die. Nothing seemed to matter, so I stopped taking care of myself and the spaces around me. In this state, even everyday chores can seem as daunting as climbing a mountain. I wondered, how could I shake myself out of this frame of mind?

I started doing what I'd done from the very beginning: making daily to-do lists. These included everything from making the bed to brushing my hair and washing my face. One by one, I'd check off each item. This helped my mountains of chores begin to feel more manageable and enforced a sense of structure around my days. Now, I had a routine to operate within, and with time and repetition, this habit helped me feel normal. All I had to do was check each item off the list, and a sense of relief and encouragement would flow through me, however small. I was accomplishing things, and little by little, I was able to add more and more tasks to the list.

Put on makeup. Flat iron my hair. Paint my nails. Iron my clothes. Organize my closet. Get out of my PJs, and put on some different clothes.

Over time, the list grew to include the kinds of tasks that challenged me to get out of the darkness of my bedroom and find my way into the light.

Go for a walk. Go outside and do a fun activity. Make new friends. Learn to trust people again.

Journaling doesn't have to be limited to making lists: eventually, I even used my journal to write the first draft of this book.

Tip #3: Find Your Inspiration

"If you don't like something, change it. If you can't change it, change your attitude."

—Maya Angelou

If you are fortunate to have a support system made up of individuals in your day-to-day life, then by all means, use it. Talk to them. Lean on them. If you don't have the support of family, friends, or professionals, it is still entirely possible, as I've learned, to motivate yourself. At times when I've been at my most stressed and depressed, and was at a loss for how to accept myself, sticky notes became my savior. Well, not sticky notes alone, but the motivational and inspirational quotes that I scribbled on hundreds of the adhesive notecards.

I collected the sayings from anywhere and everywhere. Anything that kept me going, I wrote down. If a message spoke to me, I used it. I even created some of my own. They all found their way onto sticky notes, and I stuck them everywhere. On my mirror. On my books. On my computer. In my car. I kept them visible at all times, because they truly helped me. Slowly, over time, their messages seeped into my conscious mind, and then into my subconscious mind. Now, they are a part of who I am.

There are many books and websites dedicated to such quotes. I have also created a whole page on my website just to share a few that helped me, and the list is still growing. Find them. Use them. Sticky notes have become such an important part of my routine, and I'm grateful for the role they've played in helping me to get organized, to feel inspired, and to transform into the person I want to be.

Whether you use sticky notes, or something else that works for you, be your own advocate and make inspiration a part of your daily routine.

Tip #4: Keep Busy

"It takes a lot of courage and trust to look past what you've been through, and trust someone new not to put you through it again."

—Kaniz Fatima Lily

Sure, this is easy to say but hard to find the energy to do. Nevertheless, getting out of bed was one of the best things I did for myself every day. Whether I was afraid of my abuser, down on myself because I was believing the verbal assaults, depressed about my circumstances, or in physical pain, having places to be and or things to get done propelled me out of my misery.

This tip is especially important for anyone experiencing negativity within their own home. In addition to the physical abuse, I was constantly absorbing destructive messages in the household— that I was worthless or that it would have been better if I'd died in the car crash or in the shooting. I couldn't permanently escape my home at the time, but I purposefully set out to spend very little time there. I encourage you to do the same if it's the source of your trauma.

Getting myself into a steady routine made a world of difference. Small rituals like waking up early, going to the gym, cooking, going to work or class, doing my homework, assisting with housework, polishing my to-do lists, and arranging my daily outfits one night early all gave me motivation to look forward to the next day.

By putting myself out there and socializing—at work, at gatherings, volunteering at election campaigns—I got to meet new people. Slowly, I noticed that everyone was struggling with their own demons, like me. I wasn't alone. In the past, I'd met many people who were willing to engage with me about my struggles, but at the time, I was too scared to open up to them. Once I began making positive changes in my life, however, I got back in touch with some of my old friends and extended family members who had tried reaching out to me before. I realized these people could have been a wonderful support system, had I known how to identify and utilize their support. Sometimes when we're suffering, we close our minds and hearts to those trying to help. Don't let your trauma blind you to any avenues of support that may be available; the compassion we need may be closer than we think. Reach out to your contacts, old and new alike. I want to thank all those who stuck by me and never gave up, even when I didn't have the tools to let them into my life.

The more I got out and interacted, the more people began opening up to me about their problems, too, and encouraging me to share with them about mine. Some very sympathetic and caring connections formed between us. Here I was, surrounded by people who were willing to take time to listen, and it was OK that they were not my family and that we didn't share the same traits, cultural or religious. We understood each other, and just like that, I realized how it is possible to learn to trust others again. I had proof.

It doesn't matter what you do, as long as it's a healthy option that quiets the mind and bolsters your confidence. Go to school. Get a job. Volunteer. Walk a dog. Join a club, a team, or a gym. Write a book. Whatever gets you up each day and gives you a focus outside your suffering.

Tip #5: Make Life Bigger Than Your Immediate Circumstances

"Forgive others, not because they deserve forgiveness, but because you deserve peace."

—Jonathan Lockwood Huie

While my traumas have been severe, I'm greater than the sum of them. By training myself to look beyond the borders of my pain, I've learned to focus on the bigger picture—the things that lie outside the territory of my traumas and shed completely different light on my life story.

One way I started studying the bigger picture was by analyzing the lives of others who had made it out of misery, too. I took note of some of their habits and adopted them as my own: eating better, exercising, taking "me" time, reading, going to sleep early and getting an early start to the day, and sticking to a routine. I joined a gym and took up yoga. I went on a lot of walks.

Another thing I did to broaden my horizon was I started cooking again, something I hadn't done for many years. I looked up different recipes and tried making a new dish two or three times each week. This took my attention completely off of my problems, gave me something to look forward to, and connected me with a joyful part of myself I hadn't indulged in for a while. It even gave me an opportunity to bond with my nieces and other family members who got involved. Others were joining in my passion, collaborating with it, strengthening their relationships with me. This helped me begin to feel more "normal" again, like I was a part of something positive, something larger than my pain.

My story is far from over. I'm alive and finding my way forward in places where my voice is valued. I'm speaking up about what I've lived through in the hopes that it will inspire others to share their stories, too. Every day, I'm engaging with passions and activities that unite others with me, bring me joy and boost my energy, and remind me that my pain is only one portion of my story. There is no better way for me to fight for survivors' rights than by finding purpose in my suffering. Don't let abuse and trauma define you. It is something happening *to* you, not *because* of you. And it is not all of you. There is so much more to your life, to your story. You must believe that your purpose is far more important than what you may be going through at the time.

Tip #6: Save Money

"Price is what you pay. Value is what you get."

—Warren Buffett

I know how hard things can be, but no matter what, it is important to put aside a few dollars here and there, even if it's no more than one dollar a day, to get in the habit of saving. This enables us to be prepared for unforeseen circumstances.

When I first moved out of my family's house, I was relieved and thrilled to be able to use the money I'd saved up over the years to make myself independent and comfortable. Then, when I got a new job, I started saving right away again, giving me power to do what I liked! This level of freedom was encouraging.

My advice is to set a goal for yourself, based on where you reside. Calculate your expenses and estimate how much money you may need if something was to go wrong. A good rule of thumb is to save for at least three months of living expenses at all times. To decrease your spending, try writing down everything—yes, everything—you buy and consume for two weeks. Choose two weeks out of your regular life, as opposed to traveling or vacation. Then, analyze your list to brainstorm areas for cutting back. This helps you track your spending, but also changes your perspective on where your money goes. Money won't solve your problems, but exercising financial self-discipline prepares you for worst-case scenarios and grants you a healthy form of freedom that improves your life.

It also gives you a kind of power: when people know you're independent, they respect you and take you seriously. There have been times when my family understood that due to my lack of financial independence, I was vulnerable and defenseless. But after the shooting, when I was threatening to take legal action against them, the fact that I had a savings account put some fear into them. Even though I didn't have enough money to cover my many medical expenses, they still knew I had enough to hire a lawyer to destroy them. If I hadn't had any money saved at that time, I would not have had a leg to stand on during those negotiations, which would have given them the upper hand. Thanks to this, I was able to get over

$200,000 from them to cover medical expenses. Later, I even saved up money to publish this book, and it means a lot to me to be able to give it away for free to help others.

Bonus Tip: Seek Professional Help

"If you don't heal what hurt you, you will bleed on people who didn't cut you."

—Rumi

Lastly, seeking professional help from a psychotherapist or counselor should be included among your recovery strategies.

Even though I haven't had the opportunity to take advantage of this option as much as I'd like, it's a viable resource and available to most. People can be stuck in their ways. If they have a negative perception of you, then it's not always worth your energy to try to change it. Rather than using your strength to fight against people's false perceptions, simply focus your resources on taking care of your own needs. Put yourself first, and others' impressions will fall by the wayside.

Sometimes, just by connecting with others and sharing hard-earned wisdom, we can chart a path outside our own pain. I encourage you to join, or form, your own community. A little goes a long way. Connect with others, even if it's as simple as sharing your techniques with people already in your life or seeking out new people with whom you can exchange tips.

If you need help getting started, you're welcome to explore the Communication Board on my website, IramGilani.com, where you'll have the opportunity to read others' suggestions and post your own. This board is not solely for people whose lives have been affected by trauma. It's a platform for anyone and everyone, whether suffering or not, to join in the conversation, receive and offer support, and exchange insights via messages and comments. The idea is to connect with others in whatever way works best for you. Start your own conversations with those who make you feel safe.

6
Support is Critical

"To be kind is more important than to be right. Many times, what people need is not a brilliant mind that speaks but a special heart that listens."

—F. Scott Fitzgerald

Along with sharing my story to inspire others who have suffered abuse and trauma, it's just as important to me to educate non-sufferers. Hopefully, the previous chapters have illuminated some aspects of the behaviors and emotions that survivors may experience, so non-sufferers can better understand what others may be going through. One thing that can make all the difference to a person struggling with trauma is the support that he or she receives. And, it is entirely possible to do this even if you haven't had personal experience with trauma, yourself. You can still learn how to understand it and to offer comfort. Your effort is critical to helping survivors recover.

When you see someone who has been abused, you may not be sure how to treat that person. It's common and understandable to be afraid you may say or do something to offend them. You may worry you have inadequate knowledge or nothing of value to share. There are a lot of *what-ifs* and *I-don't-knows* in these circumstances. But simply starting a conversation can make a world of difference. Openly speaking to survivors about their issues is, in and of itself, a form of support. And while feeling apprehensive is normal, I want to help eliminate it so that more conversations and connections can form.

When I was in high school and college, I reached out to very few people because I thought they didn't understand me. I'm sure I'm not alone, because evidence shows many victims of abuse are introverts who tend to keep to themselves and have limited support systems. There are many people who tend to be quiet and reserved, and it's easy to spend a night with a group of friends and say very little out loud. It's not that they don't have opinions or comments to add to the conversation, but they may not have loud personalities. Something I know about myself is that if I'm not engaged by others, then I don't push to engage with them myself. This is especially true when it comes to emotional issues and or personal needs. There are many people, especially trauma survivors, who relate to this.

However, this isn't to say that I didn't look for support; in my case, I just didn't find it. Or at least, I didn't find anything that read to me as genuine concern. Even after the shooting, when I was recovering from a trauma that was very visible, I sensed a distinct absence of consistent sympathy from those around me. Every now and then, someone would ask how I was doing, which I appreciated, but the conversations didn't get very far. This is common, too: people may ask a survivor how they're feeling, but then begin finishing the survivor's sentences for them, trying so hard to sympathize that they inadvertently take away the survivor's voice in the dialogue. Or, they'll start talking about themselves, so eager to relate to the survivor's experiences that the conversations swing towards their own thoughts and feelings, instead.

Worse yet are the clichéd comments, which originate from a good place, but can come across as shallow. At times when you are at your most depressed and struggling the most with a painful situation, you may find yourself feeling irritated with overly happy and positive people. There were times when I couldn't even watch comedies on television, because it made me angry. I was suffering so much that happiness seemed like a lie. Others' feelings were simply so far from where I was at the time, that it drew my attention to my own loneliness.

Occasionally, someone with good intentions would say, "Cheer up. It's going to be okay." There is no way they could have guessed the impact it would have on me, but these kinds of commonplace statements can be very painful. They stir up a lot of feelings about trauma and tap into survivors' wounds.

The problem is that clichés make it sound easy to recover, as though happiness is right at everybody's fingertips, and survivors could reach right out and grab it if they really wanted. This often unintended message can be hurtful and irritating. Empty adages can cause trauma survivors to feel more alone in their suffering. Offering platitudes, or feigning interest, can make people feel worse instead of better.

The key is sincerity. If you care for someone who has been traumatized, reach out and engage them in meaningful conversations in which you give them a chance to speak, and you truly listen. If your concern comes across in a genuine way, then survivors will feel seen and heard. It takes more than a pre-packaged, positive statement to touch the heart of someone who has been through a lot in life. To help pick up a person you love from the floor, you have to lean down and offer them a hand, because those suffering may not have the energy to meet the person otherwise. *They need you more than anything.*

Once you've opened a conversation, hold the person's trust with active listening. Look them in the eye. Be attentive and engaged. Quiet your mind about saying the "right" thing and really listen to their words. Reflect back and summarize what you heard the person say. You don't need to solve their problems. Just make them feel understood and that their feelings are valid and their problems matter. Don't push them to share anything they're uncomfortable talking about, but, at the same time, don't be afraid to ask questions. Let them set the boundaries for discussing their most sensitive stories.

Before the shooting, people assumed I had a perfect life, because I always presented myself in a friendly manner, with a smile on my face. Suppressing true feelings is one of the hardest things anyone can do, because you may be smiling on the outside, but you're hurting on the inside. You're silently screaming for help, hoping that someone sees past the fake smile and asks you how you're really doing. I wasn't fortunate enough to have anyone see my pain, but no matter who I met, I always wanted to know all about them: their interests, the things they liked and disliked, etc. Their answers were clues for me on how to appear "normal." If someone said, "I go running in my spare time!" or "I read a lot of books," or "I watched a movie last night," then I borrowed these responses as my own during conversations in order to feel more inclusive. The truth was that during the last five to seven years, I didn't have time to do "normal" things like read books, watch movies, or hang out with friends, because I was working full-time and studying full-time. But I believed that if someone asked me how I was doing, and I told them the truth about my feelings, they would find me to be awkward or feel uncomfortable, themselves. Instead, I chose to go with the flow. I kept my true self from being seen to fit in among others.

In my heart, I lived in the world I pictured in my head: one where there was no violence or abuse, where everyone loved each other and got along, and where people actually cared and provided support to each other. I replaced my painful reality with this imaginary one, inventing fake stories about how wonderful and supportive my family was, and how lucky I was to be wearing the brands I wore and going where I wanted. In reality, I didn't have any of that. I just wanted to fit in, and pretending that I was happy enabled me to keep a smile on my face. The truth was, I'd found a way to live in an imaginary world, and that imaginary world actually distanced me from people who were available to connect with me in real life.

After the shooting, I hid away for the first few years, only going out to doctor appointments and eventually back to school. When I did go out in public, I'd avoid most people and conversations. But now that I'm more comfortable, I've noticed that most people talk to me by looking at my scars. For anyone who has visible evidence of their trauma, this can happen a lot. People don't look directly into our eyes. It's clear they must be speculating and forming assumptions, yet they're not asking any questions directly.

As a result, it can be hard to tell whether the other person is really listening when you share your story. They may try to make small talk, but their minds are elsewhere. Whether they realize it or not, this can make the other person feel very self-conscious. I'll think, *if you want to know what happened, why not just ask?* It's OK that people are curious about each other's injuries. And by asking about them directly, people have an opportunity to share their own stories, in their own voices. This could be a start to building mutual trust and respect—a chance to form a meaningful connection.

Of course, this isn't always appropriate. There are times when a person on the subway or standing next to me in a store line glances my way and sees my scars. That happens, and it's normal for a stranger not to ask questions. But if I'm interacting with someone, whether in class or with a cashier at a grocery store or meeting someone new at a party or event, and there's an opportunity to open up a deeper kind of conversation, then don't just stare. Reach out. Open up a dialogue. Build a shared understanding.

I can't speak for everyone with visible scars and deformities. However, I am sure I speak for everyone when I say don't stare, because that's painful for us all. If it's gotten to that point, and the situation becomes awkward, it's best to acknowledge it. That doesn't necessarily mean a person needs to ask questions. If that's uncomfortable, simply offer a smile while looking the person in the eye instead. Treat everyone, whether they are survivors or not, the same way; with acceptance and kindness. Boost their self-esteem and confidence by making them feel normal and that they belong.

When someone is abused or experiences a traumatic event, their perception of self is often skewed. They no longer look in a mirror and see anything but bruises or scars. Or, if it's invisible pain, they believe people can see their secret. They may think they're damaged, no longer like others.

That is why acceptance, inclusion, and positivity is so critical. Survivors see themselves through the eyes of others. When you meet someone who is struggling, and you look away instead of holding their eye-contact, that person may feel their self-esteem dropping. Focusing on their struggles can distract you from the person they really are. But when you start a discussion, inviting another person to share reminds everybody we're all equals. And if someone else says, "you're beautiful, you're strong, you're courageous," then its impact is significant. All of us, no matter what we've been through, take a great deal of cues from how others react to and perceive us.

So, no matter who you are, and with whom you're speaking, try to focus on the person, giving them attention and genuine kindness. It goes a long way.

The Power of Small Acts

"No gesture is too small when done with gratitude."

—Oprah Winfrey

Engaging communication is key. Eye-contact and listening are critical. Treating survivors normally is important. Start with these concepts, and we can provide healthy support to those who suffer the anguish, limiting beliefs, and stress of abuse and trauma. But support goes beyond just listening. Take the time to *do* things, as well.

I'm not asking people to put their lives on hold to help others. I'm encouraging people to take the time to acknowledge those who may be suffering. Send a simple message saying, "I'm thinking about you." Share something funny, inviting laughter back into their lives. Share anything uplifting to boost their self-confidence and self-esteem. Simply connect with them.

After I was shot, and was going through a few surgeries, a friend sent me a song—"Scars To Your Beautiful," by Alessia Cara— affirming that not only are scars normal, but that they can add to your beauty, your strength, and your uniqueness. She said whenever she heard it played, she thought of me. That simple gesture really touched me, because it was thoughtful and encouraging, too.

If more time is available, then reach out with a phone call. Check in, but then chat about anything. If the survivor is within the same home, sit with the person. Hold their hand in quiet companionship. Watch a favorite TV show together. Invite conversation and make yourself available to them. The smaller the act of kindness, the more normalcy it creates for those suffering. We don't have to move a mountain to make a difference. A smile or hand raised in recognition can provide a survivor a lot of encouragement and help bring them back to life. Start with making them feels welcomed, included, and acknowledged. Nothing is lost when someone makes an effort, only if no effort has been made.

One last thing to consider in offering support to survivors: help guide them to resources. Many people think that being in a progressive country like America, as opposed to third and fourth world countries, makes it easier to find and access help. Unfortunately, I haven't found this to be the case. Regardless of your location, when you are suffering, you become discouraged and disheartened. You can't find the encouragement to make the positive changes you wish to make in your life. Getting assistance is not as easy as packing up some bags and relocating, and resources are more scarce than most people assume. And the resources that do exist are challenging to access.

Often, people who haven't been victims of abuse examine abusive situations from the outside and say, "If that were me, I'd just leave. I wouldn't tolerate it a bit longer." For the majority of those who have been trapped in abusive situations, however, it is not as simple as just getting up and leaving. For me, my greatest barriers to escaping were my financial restrictions, as well as my older brother. Although I did leave home once, hoping to secure some independence for myself so that I could take him with me as soon as possible, my car accident put me right back in an abusive atmosphere, and I had to restart from scratch.

All my life, my older brother has been a shield for me. He sees me as someone he can come to for anything, always remarking, "You and I are one, right?" To this day, he asks me this every chance he gets. When I was struggling to get out of a toxic household, I felt I couldn't disappoint him. I couldn't just pack my bags and leave, knowing how much he needed me, just as I needed him. I know how it feels to be neglected and abandoned, your loved ones packing up and disappearing overnight; I couldn't do this same thing to my kind and loving brother. Besides, I didn't have the means to support the two of us, and I didn't want to put him in a stressful situation that he didn't have the mental capacity to understand. These kinds of predicaments are the reason we hear of so many people suffering in silence for years before they can find a way out of an abusive situation. Not having reliable options truly hinders your ability to escape, however "intolerable" one's abusive situation may be.

At times when I was searching for resources to find a place to live, pay for surgeries, and find a free therapist, I was battling with so many other obstacles that I sometimes didn't have the energy to get out of bed in the morning, let alone search for services that would help me recover. I'd come across a website that looked like it could help, but so many times, it would turn out to be a government funded program that required me to submit all kinds of reports and verify my identity before they could offer anything. This was during a time when I didn't even know that it was trauma that I was suffering from. I couldn't name my condition—how could I seek out the resources to treat it? A few well-intentioned friends would occasionally send me a link to a website, but then leave it to me to follow up.

When a person is traumatized, they may not know what they're looking for or how to find it. So, be their compass. Find resources for them. Encourage them to call, or better yet, help them make that first call. Support them as they venture to gain their equilibrium.

7

Meet in the Middle

"I believe we can all come together, because if you take away the labels, you realize we're far more alike than we are different."

—Ellen DeGeneres

After the gunshot incident, I barely spoke with my family for an entire year. I was focused on my recovery. I forgave my family for what had happened, with the hope of finding a new beginning, asking only that they never betray me again. My parents promised no one would ever lay a hand on me again, and so, with a combination of faith in them and honor in our family name, I once again complied with their wishes.

But when my younger brother, with his wife and daughter, returned from Pakistan to live in our family's home in the U.S., life became challenging again. Given what had happened, living together under the same roof was far from easy. Honestly, it was something I'd never imagined having to do. But I was willing to sacrifice some of my personal comfort if it meant keeping the peace for the entire household. For a short time, things were calm. We were getting along. But then, my younger brother began displaying outbursts of anger again. The tension grew, escalating to arguments with my parents about how unsafe I felt in our home. Since I was still recovering, I didn't have the ability to move into my own place, so I had no choice but to stay there. My brother and his wife, on the other hand, knew the impact of their presence on me. They had the option to move someplace else, but they chose not to.

It was around the end of June, 2016, when my younger brother attempted to attack me, again. If it were not for my older brother and father intervening, he may have killed me. My parents instructed me to stay in my room until he calmed down. But that night, a sense of terror and dread overcame me. I understood my safety was truly at risk, and that, unless I took action, my death might be the only possible outcome.

The next day, my older brother and I drove to see the magistrate judge of the Prince William County (PWC) to obtain a temporary restraining order against my younger brother and his wife. After listening to what my older brother and I had to say, the magistrate immediately issued the order. I hoped that my parents would understand my fear and show support in my obtaining legal protection for myself. Instead, they were furious, demanding that I leave the house. As soon as my younger brother returned home, my father took him to the PWC Police Station to not only overturn the restraining order, but also to issue a new one: this time, one that would protect *him* from *me.*

But the police didn't see things that way. My younger brother was served, and it was explained to my father that once the order was issued, it could not be cancelled. For three days, my brother and his wife were not legally permitted to enter the house, and for the entirety of those three days, my parents were extremely upset with me. When the three of us—me, my brother, and his wife—were to appear in court so that I could request an extension or permanent restraining order, my parents came with us.

Their goal was not to offer support, but rather, to take the opportunity to falsely claim that I was lying about my brother's attack. To my horror, they even lied to the judge about my older brother's credibility: claiming he wasn't mentally competent enough to provide a truthful statement. This didn't come from a place of cruelty towards me. It came from their desire to prevent my younger brother from getting into deeper trouble, such as going to jail. They were willing to protect him, even if that meant covering up my attempted murder. This was painful. Most of us count on our families for love and support. Standing up for my brother over me—knowing he was guilty—created a distance between us, filled with hatred.

Once my younger brother and his wife were permitted to return to my parents' house, he began to taunt me, making me feel unsafe in my home, yet again. The mood in the house was tense for everybody, my parents included. To cope with this, they told me to leave. I was given 30 days to move out.

At this point, I was fully dependent on them financially. I'd been focusing on my constant surgeries and trying to recover. With the clock ticking, however, I applied to George Washington University, praying I'd get in. Thankfully, I was accepted, and I was overjoyed to have a positive incentive for moving out.

That didn't make it easy, though. I arrived on campus with no family support, not even a quick phone call to check in and find out how I was doing. I only had one credit card with an $800 balance. Initially, while trying to adjust, I used some of the funds to buy my books and pay for other expenses, but within a few short months, I was running out of money. I knew I needed to find a job—and fast. Despite my depression and lack of support, I began applying for jobs and was relieved when I was able to begin working. Completing school was my main goal, and I was willing to do everything I could to make it happen. It felt as though completing my degree was my only way out of a bad situation, and that it would secure my and my older brother's future. This gave me the motivation to work hard and fulfill my course requirements as best I could. I did not want to quit under any circumstances.

The loneliness I felt during this time was unspeakable. But, as shaken as I was, I was equally open to this new, inviting experience in a whole new change of scenery, and with a brand-new group of people. It was like starting fresh. One thing I hoped to find there was a sense of stability, a community to help me recover from the chaos of my family life back at home. Another thing I hoped for was an opportunity to expand my own horizons, to find a sense of belonging I'd never experienced.

Washington D.C. is a thriving city. It has a unique spirit, made possible by the synthesis of people from every culture, background, and experience imaginable. It is like no other: not only because of the central political powers residing there, but also due to the intersections of people, passionately fighting to make the world beyond themselves a better place.

Eager to find ways to become a part of the campus, I searched for organizations at the university to join. Although I did not fit the profile of the typical college student, I still hoped to find people who were compassionate, eager to embrace those different from themselves, and open to forming new and meaningful connections, one of the most rewarding life experiences there is.

Unfortunately, I soon learned that many students were segregated into groups of people similar to themselves. As an outsider to their inner circles, I felt unwelcome. This was painful for me, having come from an environment where I already did not feel welcome. Further, I couldn't help but feel that many of the other students stared at me. After the shooting, when I returned to community college, the environment felt familiar: many of the students knew me from before, and I was already accustomed to the campus. George Washington University, on the other hand, was a different world, where I was a stranger.

Still struggling to find my way and cope with ongoing neglect, I would spend a lot of spare time trying to find motivation and support. While watching a video, I heard Dr. Gary Parker talking about deformities. "The uniform that's put on people when you have these horrible deformities is: You're rubbish. You're worthless. You're spiritually cursed. And when you can change the uniform it's huge. And the person starts to imagine that they might not be rubbish after all. No one in our world is rubbish," he said. *He's right,* I thought. Finishing school was important to me. Instead, I began thinking of ways that I could fix the problems I was encountering. Wasn't there any place on campus where I could belong?

The truth was that many other students on this campus felt the same way. My experience of feeling alone and disconnected from my community was actually a sentiment shared by many other students, not only at the

George Washington University, but at university campuses worldwide. GWU places a strong emphasis on students' independence, which promotes responsibility; but for students who are highly dependent by the time they arrive on campus, this can add to their feelings of isolation. This push towards independence, coupled with its busy urban setting, could make the campus feel like a lonely place.

I also began to notice the importance of communication in connecting people. Everyone I knew was going through something, whether it was relationship issues or family issues. Instead of opening up with them about my own problems, I sometimes found myself holding back, because I didn't want to burden them any further with my own needs. I wanted to be there for them and help relieve, rather than add to, their stress.

This is where good listening skills can sometimes hinder rather than nurture a connection: many people fall into the trap of suppressing their own feelings in exchange to take on the weight of others'. Holding back, even for well-intentioned reasons, can limit a friendship. And truly good listening doesn't just stop once a person finishes telling their story; to really understand someone, there needs to be more. Anytime someone says they "understand what I went through," it hurts. Unless they've walked in my shoes, they couldn't possibly understand. But listening to me share my story is a start, a way for them to try. And healthy communication thrives on reciprocity, where both parties show their true selves. It's that give-and-take of time, compassion, and stories that can forge lasting bonds.

Today, the difficulty in connecting with others can be compounded by the rise of social media. Now, it's more common than ever to make assumptions about others without really listening to them and understanding where they're coming from: all you have to do is look at a single picture, and you can make some harmful assumptions about a person's life. And these images, being heavily manipulated and filtered, can reinforce unrealistic standards, prompting people to have negative images of themselves, through comparison. Immersing ourselves in images of others is a way of immersing ourselves in an alternate reality, where a level of enhancement is considered so normal that beauty standards rise to impossible levels. In this way, many of the most successful celebrities and influencers can create confusion for everybody else about what beauty really is, especially the younger generation, whose self-esteem is still fragile and forming. Even those of us with the healthiest self-esteem can struggle to feel whole, or worthy of others' acceptance, when we compare ourselves to others on a purely superficial level.

By proliferating the ease of judgment without communication, social media platforms also provide easy access to anonymous harassment. In this climate, it is crucial that we take the time to see beyond appearance and try to appreciate everybody's unique past and circumstances.

This problem did not begin with social media, but, rather, exists in every platform on which we perceive and judge others without bothering to truly understand their entire stories. The homeless, for example, are often perceived as drug addicts, when, in reality, there are many reasons people find themselves on the streets. Or, a person struggling with a substance addiction is judged for not trying hard enough to quit, when often, substance abuse is complicated by mental illness, abuse, or PTSD. No one is immune to these kinds of challenges, and yet, the price of judgment can be the difference between life and death. The best start to helping each other heal is taking the time to listen to each other's stories.

Creating Change

"Turn your wounds into wisdom."

—Oprah Winfrey

Disheartened by my own experience of trying to fit in at the George Washington University, I wondered: was there anything I could do? As I saw it, students were either part of activities and groups at the university, or they weren't part of anything. I thought there was a large gap between the two. Particularly, I saw a lot of students who didn't quite fit into the "norm" of society, some of whom did not speak English very well, being isolated. They hadn't engaged with clubs or other organizations on campus. What if there could be an organization on campus where they could feel that they belonged?

I sent a questionnaire out, mostly to international students and got their input, so it wasn't all from my own experiences that I conceived the organization. It wasn't meant for any one marginalized group, like those who have suffered abuse or foreigners or LGBTQ. The idea was simply to connect anyone who felt excluded, enabling the to connect with one another and to feel that they, too, were part of something valuable. I initiated conversations with peers and got about seven of us together. Meet in the Middle was born.

Meet in the Middle, as I envisioned it, would be an organization for those who felt cast aside from the mainstream student body. In such a divided campus, I wanted there to be a true middle ground, where people with all kinds of life experiences could unite, forging a sense of community through communication.

My thought was to plan monthly activities rather than just meetings. The idea was to go out for pizza and a movie, have coffee together and chat, do a clothing drive for a local shelter, etc. The activities were all in an effort to build relationships and include time for members to share about themselves. Connecting people goes back to the fundamental idea of supporting each other. And I wanted to offer it to my classmates who seemed to be lacking it.

Meet in the Middle had some success early on, but the group dwindled as initial members graduated, and founding an entire campus organization proved a challenge for my schedule, as I was working over 40 hours a week while going to classes as a full-time student, and dealing with another round of surgeries at the same time. So, it never became an official George Washington University organization. The silver lining is that this allows me to resurrect it on my own now.

This experience left me with a strong desire to work with schools and other organizations so that I can provide a place where all kinds of people—regardless of their life experience—can start a conversation, exchanging support and encouragement. I want to promote change by encouraging people to take the time to get to know someone beyond the image they perceive from a cursory view. Start a conversation. Learn a person's story. And, at the very minimum, if a person is not willing to invest the time to get to know someone's journey, then don't make assumptions and be judgmental. By simply communicating, we can learn to understand one another's differences and accept each other. Students, in particular, could benefit from this kind of space, as campuses can be so divided. This has become my dream, and my goal, for the future: to create a positive change by bringing people together.

Only the Beginning

"With faith, discipline, and selfless devotion to duty, there is nothing worthwhile that you cannot achieve."

—Muhammad Ali Jinnah

Going forward, I plan to build on the foundation of Meet in the Middle, creating a platform for people to find support and share useful resources. My mission is to coordinate with organizations to find a clear path for people to access useful resources. It will be for anybody seeking to connect with others, whether you are a survivor of abuse and trauma, or a loved one of a person who could use your support. It will be a kind of home for anyone who feels alone or isolated.

Rather than simply making resources available, I hope to find ways to speak out about the importance of support and be an advocate for others, sharing different techniques as I continue to learn them. I hope to work with organizations to find real solutions for those who have been impacted by abuse and trauma, so I can guide people, step by step, towards obtaining the care they need. Support of any kind is valuable, but useful assistance is essential for survivors, who, as a result of what they're struggling with, could benefit from extra assistance in accessing treatment. There are many organizations, groups, and therapists that could help a person recover, but, at the same time, insurmountable obstacles can stand in their way. My hope is to help guide survivors past those obstacles, so that nobody has to feel stuck without help.

As an aspiring founder of my own organization, I'm still learning as I go. Although my vision is rooted in a lifetime of experience, in many ways, I'm just getting started. And this book is the first step—ideally, the first of many more books to come. It's been my effort to not only share my story, but to connect with others who have survived the life-changing effects of trauma, too.

In it, I've encouraged readers to examine the broader scope of abuse, recognizing the greater forces that drive all of our actions, and that each instance of trauma is its own intricate portrait—it is rarely as simple as "perpetrator versus victim," and each person involved has his or her own story worth hearing. I've encouraged loved ones and caregivers to learn the signs of abuse and trauma and have shared with them some ways in which they can be supportive: communication is the key to understanding others, opening the door to compassion and acceptance. I want readers to understand that I do not blame anyone in this book for the things I've struggled with. The goal has not been to gain sympathy or elicit anger towards the people in it. I wrote this book to share the positive outcomes of my challenges so that readers can use them as inspiration to overcome their own circumstances.

I am grateful that God chose for me to walk this journey. That He believed in me and gave me the strength to keep moving in the right direction. We are all put on this earth for a purpose, each of us perfect in our own ways because we were created by God, and He does not make mistakes. I hope for as many chances as possible to fulfill the purpose God has planned for me, to satisfy my responsibilities as a human before my time is up.

I believe in the good intentions of others, even when I have not agreed with their actions, or when those actions have caused me pain. Each incident I've gone through has made me a better person, and although no one should ever choose to suffer, the rewards of surviving challenges are gaining more tolerance, acceptance, and a greater understanding of others as well as ourselves.

To keep this in perspective, take care to understand the underlying issues of any traumatic situation. Blaming someone is often the easiest route, but look beyond that and consider why people in your life may have behaved in certain ways. You will see that all of us, even the perpetrators of abuse or crime, are battling our own demons and often screaming for help. Blaming others creates barriers and hateful distance, but empathy builds a bridge, and the truth is, we need each other to feel complete. We all make mistakes, and learning to forgive others, even when they don't act in your best interests, creates bonds and teaches us to be kind and forgiving towards ourselves.

Learn to embrace and uplift each other, empowering one another to achieve your destinies as God's gifts. If you've gained anything from this book, I hope it's this message of acceptance, forgiveness, and unity.

I pray that by sharing my personal experiences, others will be inspired to reach out to me, knowing that I can understand some, or many, elements of their battles. I've fought my own, in my own shoes, with my own tools. But together, perhaps we can win the fight.

Join me in finding hope together at IramGilani.com

Epilogue: *No More Lives Lost*

"The world is better with you in it."

—Rajdeep Sinha

To all survivors here and gone,

For those of you who are no longer with us, who believed that committing suicide was your only way out of your misery, I want you to know that we are sorry. We couldn't see your pain in time to offer the support that would have saved your lives, and for that, we failed you.

Please know that your lives were valuable, were full of beauty and meaning. Please know that you did deserve our support. Please believe me when I say, I wish we could have given it to you.

For those of you still struggling to survive today, I want you to know that you are not alone, and that there is hope. No matter how hard life is, there is always the possibility of a new door opening, of new relationships blooming and flourishing. You can find the strength to overcome all your obstacles, especially if you take full advantage of the support that is available to you. Reach out for help. Talk to others, and show them your true selves. Make friends and join communities that can hold you when you are at your most vulnerable. Learn to trust again. I know how hard it can be.

But my promise to you is, it's worth it.

With love,

Iram Gilani

You are
BRAVER
than you believe,
STRONGER
than you seem,
SMARTER
than you think, &
LOVED
more than you'll ever know.

—Alan Alexander Milne
(18 January 1882 – 31 January 1956)

Acknowledgments

Editor

Gwyn Knauer

Co-Editor

Madeline Glackin

Logo Designer

Varun Davera

Photographers (Cover Photo)

Asad Khan

Umar Farooq

Make-Up Artist (Cover Photo)

Lisa Deverey

(by Charlotte Tilbury)

Book Design / Printed By

Profile Printing Publishing

(Islamabad, Pakistan)

Thank you to all those who have given their time and talent to helping me make this book possible. I am eternally grateful for your dedication and support throughout this process.

All services for this publication were paid for by Iram Gilani.